W9-AGW-664

Missed Periods

and Other Grammar Scares

How to Avoid Unplanned and Unwanted Writing Errors

Jenny Baranick

Skyhorse Publishing

Skyhorse Publishing books may be purchased in bulk at special discounts for sales promotion, corporate gifts, fund-raising, or educational purposes. Special editions can also be created to specifications. For details, contact the Special Sales Department, Skyhorse Publishing, 307 West 36th Street, 11th Floor, New York, NY 10018 or info@skyhorsepublishing.com.

Visit our website at www.skyhorsepublishing.com.

10 9 8 7 6 5 4 3 2 1

Library of Congress Cataloging-in-Publication Data is available on file.

ISBN: 978-1-61608-370-0

Printed in the United States of America

Table of Contents

Acknowledgments

I would love to take all the credit for the existence of this book, but the truth is it wouldn't exist without many wonderfully supportive people. Melinda Combs and Holly Vance, the members of my writing group GLOW (Gorgeous Ladies of Writing; yes, we're humble), not only endured countless drafts of grammar lessons; they provided me with their invaluable feedback and encouragement. Emily Teeple must have done something terrible in her past life because karma put her desk right in front of my office, *literally* transforming her into my unofficial proofreader. (Emily hates when people misuse *literally*.) Jeremy Aoun spent many a morning coffee listening to a highly caffeinated me ramble on and on about grammar. He also provided wonderful feedback and cooked delicious meals for GLOW. Rick Newman, Alicia Ladenes, and Danielle McConnell read early drafts of the book, and their encouragement propelled me to continue. My sister Maggie helped me tremendously with my Missed Periods and Other Grammar Scares blog. I'd like to thank my mom; my dad; my brother, Matthew; my bestie, Tricia; the FIDM staff; and all my friends and family for all of the support and enthusiasm. Thank you to everyone who has read and supported the Missed Periods and Other Grammar Scares blog. Your comments gave me confidence in my writing voice. And thank you to my agent Neil Salkind for your invaluable support and optimism and my editor Lilly Golden for being such a delight to work with.

Introduction: Confidence Is Sexy

In addition to bearing Johnny Depp's children, I always dreamt of becoming a college professor. I envisioned the day when I would lead my class of eager students in a discussion about the recurring imagery in Shakespeare or the devastatingly beautiful language that drips off the page of a Toni Morrison novel. So I received a BA and an MA in English, and although I am not Mrs. Depp, I am now actually a college professor.

Hold the applause, please. I'm not *that* kind of English professor. Unlike Robin Williams' character in *Dead Poets Society*, my lesson plan will never inspire students to sneak into the woods at night to read poetry or stand on their desks to salute me as their *Captain*. In fact, I would seriously worry about the student who found my class *that* inspiring. I am the English teacher who teaches the "boring stuff"— I teach a class on grammar called Writing Skills.

My students think I love grammar. That just says one thing to me: I chose the wrong profession— I should have been an actress. I don't *love* grammar. Loving grammar is like *loving* oatmeal. It's no three-cheese omelet, but it's good for us.

So why do I persist? Am I a masochist? Maybe. Do I fear happiness? Perhaps. But more than happiness, I fear what would happen if I stopped. I *could* put down my red pen and let the students write how they claim to write best: by freely expressing themselves without all of the "stupid grammar rules." I actually think that's a beautiful concept—in theory. However, take a look at these emails from my students; this is what freedom looks like:

- I was curious to on my grade report I got the letter F by Writing Skills. I'm guessing I didn't pass the class but what I'm curious about is how? Im **hopping** its a mistake, I know Im not the best at writing, but I did all my homework accept for two assignments and I did some extra credit.I thought I atleast did ok on the finals also. Does this mean I have to pay for it all over again to?
  *(I am sure you are **hoping** it's a mistake, but I am certainly not **hopping** over to my grade book to make any changes.)*
- I couldnt make it to class today due to a Family issue. Please excepte this peragraphs that I have sent you in this email. I will be coming in to see you monday morning about the **mider**.
  *(Make it Tuesday; I have to research what a **mider** is first.)*
- hey Mrs baranick its me k_ _ _ _, again, i don't know if you got my last message but i was asking you about my F that i got in the class. I need to know **how it got to an F** because i only missed 1 assignment and that was the 75 point one. if you can please get back to me as soon as possible because i need to know if maybe their was a mistake or **whatever**.
- (*You ask "how it got to an F"? I'm going to wager it had a lot to do with your poor grammar and punctuation—or, you know, **whatever.***)

These emails were written by the same students who believe my life revolves around grammar, the very same students who know that I am responsible for their final grade. Sending these emails to their English professor pleading for a grade change is like applying for a job at PETA wearing a floor-length fur coat.

To be fair, these examples are like Jerry Springer's guests: extreme examples of human foible. However, let's be honest: who hasn't had at least one secret love child with their sister's fiancé? (Oh, you haven't? You either? Not even one?) Well then, how many of you are guilty of committing some of the writing errors made in the email examples above: haphazard capitalization, missing apostrophes, weird spelling, and questionable email etiquette?

Don't worry. It's not your fault. We live in a very confusing time for writing. Facebook is a grammar free-for-all. Instead of curling up with a good book, we now curl up with an iPad. The iPhone adds our apostrophes for us, and might I say, not always correctly: I just got into a big fight with mine when it kept incorrectly adding an apostrophe to *its*, even though I was using it possessively instead of as a contraction for *it is*. And it's not all technology's fault: our public school systems are underfunded and overcrowded.

However, having professional writing skills is crucial. Studies show that incorrect grammar, punctuation, and spelling can prevent us from getting hired and promoted. Oftentimes, people meet our writing before they meet us; our writing *is* our first impression. People read our résumés, cover letters, proposals, and emails, and that's the basis on which we are judged first. If our writing is full of grammar and punctuation errors, even though the content may be great, it's like wearing a beautifully made Prada dress that has deodorant stains.

You may think that you don't need to worry about actually learning the grammar rules because spell check and grammar check will come to your rescue. And I get it: spell check and grammar check are great. Every time I spot a red or green line in my writing, I check it out, and many times, although I hate to admit it, I *have* made a mistake. But spell check and grammar check are like vodka: they are definitely helpful but shouldn't be solely relied on to solve our problems. Let me put it this way, if spell check and grammar check were infallible, I wouldn't have a job. Spell check, for example, won't catch when I mean to use *their* but use *there* instead, because "technically" it's spelled correctly. Sometimes grammar check tells me that a sentence I've written is incomplete when it's perfectly fine. And this is actually good news: you've seen *The Matrix*; we need to stay a little bit smarter than the machines.

Although this might not be politically correct to say, I believe that some writing-skills errors are more important to correct than others. This book covers *those* errors—the ones that are most common, the ones that confuse our readers, and the ones that may cause our readers to laugh at us. This book isn't about mastering the nuances of the complex English language; it's about making a handful of simple tweaks (some that you may even know but just need to be reminded of) in order to make our writing professional so that we can land the job interview or promotion. It's not about achieving perfection. (If you get passed over for a job because you split an infinitive, are you sure you really want to work there anyway?)

Most importantly, this book is about building your writing confidence. I have hand-picked the most common, glaring errors we make. After you apply the lessons in this book, you can be confident that your writing will be up to professional standards. And really, is there anything sexier than the confidence that exudes from a grammatically correct sentence?

1

Know Thyself: Spelling

Spelling can be as elusive as the female orgasm. We spell a word, and we think, "Oooh, I think that's it. Wait . . . no. Let me just. Oh there, maybe that's it. No. Oh, I don't know . . . I'm exhausted." And then, especially if we're in a hurry, we click *send,* and off goes that email leaving us with that unsatisfied feeling.

And who can really blame us? Society hasn't exactly promoted healthy spelling exploration. We were raised with spell check. And the English language sticks to its spelling rules, such as *i before e except after c*, about as strictly as we follow the *no cell phones while driving* rule. However, until the need for correct spelling becomes as obsolete as chivalry, we must learn how to do it; otherwise, we will appear unprofessional, and people may laugh at us and, in extreme cases, have no idea what word we are trying to spell.

The Misspelling Bee

Let's play a game. Below are ten words misspelled by my students. See if you can figure out what these words are *supposed* to be.

1. Whorable
2. Thoughs
3. Scariface
4. Nicly
5. Describetion
6. Privage
7. Celeberde
8. Sapose
9. Keith Legure
10. Sicite

Now, this might be cute if these words were misspelled by first or second graders, but these are college students we're talking about here. It's not safe to go out into the real world with such poor spelling skills. Imagine writing an email to a colleague expressing that you feel *whorable* today. You might be expected to show up to that day's meeting wearing thigh-high boots and a leather miniskirt (and may be asked what you will do for $100).

I know what you're thinking: spell check will come to my rescue. Spell check is great. Use it! Please!!! But don't use it as your only form of protection. Trust me: a few stragglers always get through.

Now, don't worry; I've got some ways for you to make sure your words are spelled correctly. And the bad news is all of these things I am about to suggest take time and energy. No quick fixes here. Just what you wanted to hear, right? The good news, however, is that you won't have to make any more of thoughs whorable scarifaces.

Spelling Strategy 1: Decent Exposure

I just visited my friend, and while I was at her house, her seven-year-old daughter and her friend asked if they could do a dance performance for me. "Sure," I said. This should be cute, I thought to myself, remembering when my sister and I used to make up dances to songs by Wham and The Go-Go's.

Cute isn't quite the word I would use to describe the experience. Let's just say there should have been a pole in the middle of the room. These girls were shaking their hips, splitting their legs, and writhing around on the ground like they were auditioning for *Striptease 2: The Prequel.*

Of course, it's not their fault: they're only copying what they see Britney Spears and Lady Gaga do on MTV. But this got me thinking: because of the human tendency to emulate what we're exposed to, to counteract the whorable spelling we encounter daily on Facebook, Twitter, and blogs, we must make time to expose ourselves to writing that contains good, solid spelling, lest we start absorbing only the misspellings.

We don't have to read Shakespeare or anything fancy. (Actually, reading Shakespeare would screw up our spelling more because we'd be writing *walkedst* instead of *walked.*) But, like we take time out of the day to go to the gym to counteract the potato chips and beer and chocolate, we need to make time to read something that has actually been edited. It doesn't have to be fancy literature. Reading an article a day from *Men's Health* or *Vogue* will do the trick. There are also plenty of well-written online sources. Even celebrity gossip site TMZ contains correct spelling. And I think I recall my husband telling me that *Playboy* has some really great articles.

Spelling Strategy 2: Vanity

Have you ever shown up to school or work with your shirt on inside out or backward? I haven't. You know why? Because I spend A LOT of time in front of the mirror checking myself out. That's right; I am terribly vain. Sure, I have to endure my husband constantly yelling at me to get going, and yes, sometimes I have to sneak past my boss because I'm late to work, but at least my tag's never in the front.

Be vain about your writing. Look it over obsessively so you don't make any silly spelling mistakes. For example, I received an essay that had my name spelled as *Ms. Break Neck* instead of *Ms. Baranick.* I thought my student was trying to be funny, so next to it I wrote, "Just doing my job." When my student got her paper back, though, her face went red. She hadn't meant to write that at all; my last name was auto-corrected, and she failed to catch it. I've also received essays about *t-shits* and *pubicity*. (I know *pubicity* is *publicity* misspelled, but I like to think of it as a new word that means people who gain publicity by exposing their pubic region.)

Spelling Strategy 3: Know Thyself

Have you ever watched hour after hour of *American Idol* auditions? No? Um . . . me neither. I just happened to be flipping through the channels one day, and I caught some of it, but I swear I never watch it. But that ONE time I did watch *American Idol*, I found myself shocked by how little self-awareness most of the people who auditioned had. I mean, they were really, really pitchy, dawgs.

Surely most of us are more self-aware than the contestants who sound like a cat whose tail has just been stepped on. For example, when you aren't sure how to spell a word, don't you feel that uncertainty in your gut? The question is what do most of us do when we get that feeling? Phone a friend for guidance? Grab our pocket dictionary out of our pocket? I am going to venture that we cross our fingers that we spelled it correctly and keep going.

So, here's the big question: If we don't know how to spell a word, how can we even be expected to find it in the dictionary so we can spell it correctly?

Okay, first of all, let's not be unrealistic. Dictionaries are like vitamins and floss; we buy them and then never use them. Even I, an English teacher, a lover of words, have a huge dictionary on my desk, and I never, ever open it. Believe me, it's not because I know how to spell every word in the English language. But, when *I* don't know how to spell a word, I don't turn to Webster; I turn to Google.

How many times have you Googled something like

Matthew Mac Conaheys abbs

Then, Google asks, Did you mean: ***Matthew McConaughey's abs?***

You think to yourself, *Thanks Google. I would never have known how to spell that crazy last name; he totally should have changed it to something simpler when he got famous like Jennifer Annasstakis did when she became Jennifer Aniston. Now, take me to those abs . . .*

Google is better than the dictionary for those times when you absolutely have no idea how to spell a word. For example, a colleague called me the other day and asked me how to spell *inebriated* (true story) after all of her attempts were underlined in red. I gave her the correct spelling, and she said, "Oh, I thought it started with an *e*." (What was she, inebriated?) She would never have found it under *E* in the dictionary, but Google would have been able to help her. If she had Google searched *enebriated*, it would have asked her:

Did you mean: ***inebriated?***

Basically, Google knows what we mean to say better than we do. So, gentlemen, next time you are confused about something your girlfriend says, just type it into Google. It will know what she means. Let's try it:

I'm fine. NOTHING'S wrong!

Did you mean: ***Something is definitely wrong, but I expect you to know what it is ?***

Another reason not to rely on spell check is because it's also kind of lazy. It's like that restaurant hostess who responds to your request for a glass of water with "I'll get your server for you."

Spell check will happily do its job and check our spelling for us, but what it will not always do is alert us when we spell a word correctly but use the wrong form of it. If, for example, we incorrectly used "affect" instead of "effect," spell check glides right past it without even as much as a red line, shrugs its shoulders, and says to itself, "It's spelled correctly. My job here is done."

So while spell check is off sipping daiquiris in the Bahamas, we need to figure out a way to differentiate between these confusing words. The first step is to know thine enemies. Now, I'm going to be honest with you: we are surrounded by enemies. There are so many words in the English language that look alike and/or sound alike. The good news is that only a handful of them are lethal. By lethal, I mean that these are the ones we use all the time that really irritate our bosses or turn off prospective employers, the ones that make people snicker at our writing as they think, "Geez, didn't they learn this stuff in the third grade?" They're not complicated words, just a bit tricky. Ladies and gentlemen, meet thine enemies, the Dirty Dozen:

1. Lose/Loose
2. Lay/Lie
3. Affect/Effect
4. Suppose/Supposed
5. Use/Used
6. Accept/Except
7. Weather/Whether
8. Than/Then
9. To/Too/Two
10. There/Their/They're
11. Your/You're
12. Its/It's

Now, let's attack!

Lose/Loose

Lose: Misplace or not win

Loose: Not tight

What do Arnold Schwarzenegger, Anthony Weiner, Tiger Woods, David Letterman, Jesse James, Bill Clinton, John Edwards, Jon Gosselin, Ryan Phillippe, Mel Gibson, and Hugh Grant have in common?

They're all men and they're all cheaters.

Well, cheer up, ladies; it's not as bad as you think. A new study shows that the gender cheating gap is closing. Women are reportedly cheating almost as much as men.

Isn't that great news? I love equality!

All this sleeping around really helps me understand a phenomenon that I've been struggling to understand for quite a while. I've always known that mixing up the words *lose* and *loose* is a common error. What I could never understand was why we tend to overuse *loose.* People more often use *loose* when they should be using *lose* rather than the other way around.

Now it makes sense. Because everyone is so sexually loose, they are subconsciously expressing it when they write. Don't give yourself away through your writing. When you use the word *loose,* make sure you mean one of the following things:

Not tight-fitting:

I had to take off my wedding ring because it was too *loose.*

Imprecise:

We *loosely* adhere to our wedding vows.

Promiscuous:

Men and women are equally *loose.*

Now, if you'll excuse me, I have to let my husband out of his cage for dinner. In this promiscuous climate, I simply can't risk letting him loose.

Lay/Lie

Lay: To put or place in a horizontal position or position of rest
Lie: To assume a horizontal or prostrate position

When someone says that he or she wants to get laid, do you know what it means? Yes, it means *that*, but do you know what it says about that person? It says that the person is lazy—that he or she is just going to lie there and not do any of the work.

To understand why it means that, we must first understand the difference between *lay* and *lie.*

The difference between *lay* and *lie* is like the difference between sadism and masochism: one means doing something to someone (or something) else, while the other means doing it to oneself.

So if we think of it that way, then *lay* is the sadist—because we use it when we are putting or placing someone or something else down:

Please just *lay* the leather whip down by the handcuffs.

The leather whip is being placed down.

The reason that people who want to "get laid" are lazy is because *laid* is the past tense of *lay*. Therefore, it means they want someone else to do it *to* them.

Lie, on the other hand, is when one places oneself down:

She told him to *lie* down on the floor and bark like a dog.

In this case, he reclined himself.

Speaking of sadism, the person who created the past tense of *lie* must have been a total sadist. Guess what the past tense of *lie* is? It's *lay.* How painfully confusing is that! Maybe some examples of the past tense of *lay* and *lie* will ease the pain:

(Lay) Yesterday, he *laid* the leather whip down by the handcuffs.
(Lie) Five minutes ago, she told him to *lay* down on the floor and bark like a dog.

Or maybe some of you masochists out there like the pain.

Affect/Effect

Affect: To produce a change in
Effect: Something that is produced, a result or consequence

Before 2002, Ben Affleck was merely an Oscar-winning screenwriter and celebrated actor. However, after he and Jennifer Lopez started dating in 2002, he became something much more interesting: he became a verb. His high-profile relationship with J.Lo was largely regarded as a terrible career and reputation move, which resulted in the Urban Dictionary defining *affleck* in the following way: *to completely screw up, to ruin one's life, to make a really bad decision.*

Thus, one might say:

Ben *afflecked* when he signed on to costar in *Gigli* with Jennifer Lopez.

While this is an unfortunate association for Mr. Affleck, it's fortunate for us. Remembering that *affleck* is a verb will help us differentiate between *affect* and *effect* because, like *affleck*, which also starts with *aff*, *affect* is a verb. It means *to produce a change in*.

***Gigli* temporarily *affected* Ben Affleck's career success.**

How did it *affect* him? His three roles following *Gigli* earned him nominations for the Golden Raspberry Award for Worst Actor.

Effect, on the other hand, is a noun. It's a thing that is produced—a result or consequence.

Watching *Gigli* had a profound *effect* on me.

The *effect* was that it makes me cringe whenever I think that I will never get those 121 minutes of my life back.

Suppose/Supposed

Suppose: To consider something as a possibility
Supposed: Expected or obliged to

The fact that so many of us use *suppose* when we should, in fact, be using *supposed* is not surprising in a time when the marriage rate is at an all-time low. What's the connection? Well, this is an error that is clearly made by commitment-phobes.

Suppose without the *d* is a totally noncommittal word. When we use it, it means that we will consider something, but there's no obligation attached. *Supposed*, on the other hand, is a word that acknowledges that there is some kind of obligation attached—something that commitment-phobes hate to acknowledge.

Lacks commitment: I suppose I could marry Dan.
Acknowledges commitment: I'm supposed to marry Dan.

The word *supposed* is like another word that commitment-phobes hate: *should*. If you admit that you're *supposed* to do something, then you've acknowledged that you *should* be doing it. Therefore, a good way to remember to add the *d* in *supposed* is to remember that *should* also ends in a *d*.

Your commitment phobia is already breaking your mother's heart; don't let it ruin your grammar.

Use/Used

Use: To employ for some purpose
Used: Accustomed to/happened regularly in the past

Like *suppose* and *supposed*, the mistake we tend to make with these two words is leaving off the *d*. Consequently, we write *use* when we should be writing *used*. However, it's not commitment-phobes who make this error; it's people who refuse to move on from the past—from their glory days.

You know the type: the middle-aged guys who still tout their high school football careers and the 1980s prom queens whose five-inch bangs are still supported by Aqua Net.

Unfortunately, that was as good as it got for these people, so when these past dwellers write about their past activities, they subconsciously leave the *d* off *used* so it looks like their past is in the present.

> Incorrect: **I *use* to be the most popular guy in school, but now I am the Thursday night trivia king at the local bar.**
> Correct: **I *used* to be the most popular guy in school, but now I am the Thursday night trivia king at the local bar.**

(It's a good thing trivia doesn't involve spelling.)

Accept/Except

Accept: To receive, agree, or consent to
Except: Excluding, but

Your ex is an ass, right?

What did he or she do? Lie? Cheat? Constantly suspect *you* of cheating? Demand all your free time? Always eat the last of the ice cream? Forget your birthday? Tell you your butt looked fat in those jeans? Love the *Meet the Fockers* franchise?

In a way, we should call those exes and thank them. If they weren't such asses, we might not have a handy way to remember the difference between *accept* and *except*.

Except, which starts with *ex*, means *but*:

> **I could put up with everything *except* her insistence that we see every *Fockers* movie.**
> **I could put up with everything *but* her insistence that we see every *Fockers* movie.**

If *but* doesn't work as a replacement, then we use *accept*. Let's try it:

I simply could not *but* that she found those movies funny.

Huh? That makes no sense, so we know that *accept* is the correct form:

I simply could not *accept* that she found those movies funny.

Therefore, when you are trying to remember whether to use *accept* or *except*, remember that the one that begins with *ex* means *but*, which you will remember because *but(t)* is another word for *ass* and your ex is an ass.

Weather/Whether

Weather: Atmospheric conditions
Whether: Used to introduce the first of two alternatives

Have you noticed how obsessed we are with discussing the weather? If it's hot, we'll tell the guy on the bus next to us how hot it is, as though the sweat dripping into his eyes hadn't clued him in. We'll talk about the cold during winter, even though winter, if I'm not mistaken, is the cold season. And don't get me started on the rain.

We love discussing the *weather* so much, in fact, that when we write it is a common error to use *weather* when we should be using *whether*.

So when you write the word *weather*, stop for a moment and ask yourself—am I discussing hazy sunshine, low clouds, highs in the 80s, or anything else that describes the atmospheric conditions? If you are, carry on and use *weather*. But, if you're not, there's a 95 percent chance that you should be using *whether*.

A trick you can use to remember that weather means rain and sun and wind is this grammatically unsound sentence:

Wherever *we at*, there's *wea*ther.

The first four letters of *weather* are weat . . . we at, and no matter where we at, there will be some kind of weather, right? Get it? C'mon.

Otherwise, we use *whether*:

I'm going to talk about the weather *whether* you like it or not.

So, anyway, how 'bout that rain?

Than/Then

Than: Used when comparing
Then: At that time, next in order of time

On the outside they look the same, but on the inside, they couldn't be more different. I, of course, am referring to Elizabeth and Jessica Wakefield, the twins from the beloved *Sweet Valley High* books of many young women's youth. On the outside, they both had sun-kissed blonde hair, golden California tans, dazzling blue-green eyes, tiny dimples in their left cheeks, perfect size 6 figures, and were 5 foot 6 on the button. (Guys, stop drooling!) On the inside, however, they couldn't have been more different: Elizabeth was the nice, studious one, and Jessica was the scheming troublemaker.

It's kind of the same deal with *than* and *then*. On the outside they look exactly alike; they look like this: *th n*. It's what they have on the inside that really gives them their identity.

Than is the one we use when we are comparing. For example:

I identified more with Elizabeth *than* with Jessica.

We are comparing how much I identified with each.

But, I secretly liked Jessica more *than* Elizabeth.

We are comparing which one I liked more.

So, to make this simple, instead of memorizing all the definitions of both words, let's just agree that when we are comparing we will use *than*, but when we're not, we'll use *then*. For example:

Jessica tried to steal Todd from Elizabeth; *then*, she tried to ruin Enid's relationship.

We are not comparing anything.

Damn, I loved that scheming bitch!

So, let's access our inner Jessica and scheme. We need to come up with a trick to remember that *than* has to do with comparing. And what is that famous saying? **It's like comparing apples to oranges**. And *apples* starts with an *a*, and *than* has an *a* in the middle.

I know this trick is not as awesome as tricking your twin sister to be a candy striper so that you can meet her celebrity patient and get famous, but it's better *than* anything else I came up with.

To/Too/Two

To: (There are too many definitions; let's not worry about it.)
Too: Also or excessively
Two: Three minus one, one plus one, eight divided by four

My grandparents used to live next door to triplets. You have to remember that this was way before Octomom, so birthing three kids at once still seemed pretty impressive. Their names were Augusto, Roberto, and Marco. Augusto and Roberto were identical, and Marco was the cute one. Needless to say, we always knew which one was Marco, but Augusto and Roberto were nearly impossible to differentiate.

It's kind of the same with *to, too,* and *two*. *Two* is the Marco of the bunch; even though it's one of the triplets, we have no trouble distinguishing it. We know it means 2, and we rarely mistake it for the others. It must be that big *W* in the middle. It's deciding between *to* and *too* that gives us the most problems.

So just like my sister and I discovered that Augusto had a pointy left ear, we have to come up with some kind of trick to tell *to* and *too* apart.

Before deciding on *to* or *too*, you have to stop and contemplate whether you need two Os or one. Here's how you know:

We use *too* when we mean *also* (e.g., **I want a pointy left ear *too*.**) The extra *O* is key to remembering this meaning because imagine the second *O* attaching itself to the word saying, "I want to come too!"

We also use *too* to mean *excessively* (e.g., **But his ear is a little *too* pointy.**) The extra O is key to remembering this definition because don't you think that two Os is a little excessive?

If we don't mean *also* or *excessively*, then it's simple: we don't need the extra *O*, so we use *to*.

There/Their/They're

There: (There are too many definitions to bother with. We'll just focus on their and they're.)
Their: Belongs to them
They're: Contraction of "they are"

Remember the 1980s Christian Slater / Winona Ryder movie *Heathers*? If you've never seen it, put this book down and add it to your Netflix rotation before you forget. I'll wait.

For those of you who haven't had the pleasure, it's the best '80s high school movie EVER. In the movie, the three most popular girls in the high school are all named Heather. However, even though they share the same name and hang out with each other all the time, Heather #1 is definitely the most popular.

We could write a similar movie about *there, their, and they're*. They all share a name, but *there* is way more popular than *their* and *they're*. In fact, oftentimes we use *there* when we should be using *their* or *they're*.

I understand why we do it. *There* has a much more broad appeal than the other two. It has twelve definitions, while *their* and *they're* only have one apiece. We're just more used to *there*. But still that's no excuse to rob the other two words of their time in the spotlight (and, I don't want to give away the *Heathers* plot, but let me just say that it doesn't always end so well for the most popular one). So instead of learning all twelve definitions of *there*, let's memorize the single definitions of *their* and *they're*.

As shown above, use *their* when we want to indicate that something belongs to *them*. It shows possession.

For example, let's look at these quotes from *Heathers:*

No one at Westerberg is going to let you play their reindeer games.

(I still don't really know what reindeer games are, but they belonged to the people at Westerberg.)

*Trick: The way to remember to use *their* when indicating that something belongs to "them" is to note that *their* contains the word *heir*, and an heir possesses belongings.

But, if you're not using *their*, meaning belonging to them, you've got a tough decision to make: *there* or *they're*.

I just lied. It's actually not that tough of a decision. You just have to stop for a moment and say the two magic words: *they are*. If those words make sense in your sentence, then you use *they're* because it's simply the shortened version of *they are*. The apostrophe gives it away.

For example:

Well, it's just like *they're* people I work with, and our job is being popular and shit.

they are

(Oh, don't you miss high school?)

So, basically, when we're not referring to something that belongs to *them* (their) or shortening *they are* (they're), then we use *there.*

Let's fill in the blanks of the following passage with the correct form of there/their/they're:

1. **Veronica: This may seem like a really stupid question.**
   J.D.: ________ are no stupid questions.
2. **Veronica: You inherit five million dollars the same day aliens land on the earth and say ________ going to blow it up in two days. What do you do?**
   J.D.: That's the stupidest question I've ever heard.

Answer Key: 1. There 2. they're

Your/You're

Your: Belongs to you
You're: Contraction of "you are"

Remember in *Peter Pan* when Tinkerbell almost died because people stopped believing in fairies? Then, we all clapped our hands and brought her back to life, and we felt really good about ourselves because we saved a precious life. In a similar vein, please put your hands together for *you're.*

Or, wait; I have a better idea: just stop using *your* when you mean *you are.* If you don't, the blood of *you're* is on *your* hands.

Its/It's

Its: Belongs to it

It's: Contraction of "it is" or "it has"

Its': Does not exist. Stop using immediately!

Ladies and Gentlemen, I'd like you to meet something. This is a word that has been around for over four hundred years, but many of us are still unaware that it exists. For those of you who have never heard of it before, I'm honored to introduce you to the word *its*. *Its* means belonging to *it:*

> ***Its* is a word. We've been denying *its* existence for too long. *It's* not fair, and *it's* been very hurtful.**

existence belongs to it

it is

it has

This concludes the spelling portion of our journey. That wasn't so bad, was it? You don't have to memorize the dictionary, and you were given the go-ahead to read *Playboy*.

EXERCISE 1: GOOGLE ME THIS

Directions: The answers to the crossword clues will be commonly confused words. The clues are actual Google searches by commonly confused people.

Down

1. What if ___ born on February 29th?
3. Why do kids eat ___ boogers?
4. What can ___ a man's sperm count?
6. How ___ is your goose?
10. Why does my goldfish swim on ___ side?
11. Am I ___ to shave?
13. What's the ___ in mars?

Across

1. Is it wrong to sleep with ___ cousin?
2. Is anybody ___?
3. Why are girls better ___ boys?
5. Who ___ to live in my house?
7. Does weed make you ___ weight?
8. Is it unhealthy to drink ___ much water?
9. What are the ___ of shrooms?
10. Chuck Norris can believe ___ not butter.
12. Should I ___ down after I eat?

2

It's Complicated: One Word, Two Words, or Three Words

I remember exactly where I was when my mom shared some very heartbreaking news with me. We were perusing the shoe section of a large department store when she said, "When I was your age, we didn't have all these shoe options. We only had two: Oxfords and Mary Janes."

The horror! Only two options for shoes!

Based on my research (i.e., watching TV shows like *Leave it to Beaver* and *Mad Men*), I've come to the conclusion that it wasn't only shoe options that were limited back then; it was also relationship options. Before the free love movement of the 1960s, apparently women were expected simply to get married and have children.

Today, it's a whole different story. Although we can get married and have children, we can choose a host of other acceptable relationship paths. We can get married and choose not to have children. We can have children and choose not to be married. We can simply choose to cohabitate. We can choose to have friends with benefits.

It should come as no surprise, then, that words today also form a variety of relationships.

Friends without Benefits: when two words should not join

These are words that hang out together very often, but they swear they only like each other as friends. However, because they spend so much time together, people tend to think that they are together and, consequently, incorrectly assume they are one word rather than two.

A and *Lot*

I can understand why Americans think *a* and *lot* should put a ring on it: *a lot* means a large number of something, and we Americans are definitely known for embracing the "the more the merrier" philosophy.

Unfortunately, *alot* is just wrong. *A lot* is destined to end up like Kevin Arnold and Winnie Cooper, not Ross and Rachel.

I really wanted Kevin and Winnie to end up together; I wanted it *a lot*.

Each and *Other*

Expecting *each* and *other* to tie the knot is like expecting the same from George Clooney and his current fling. It's simply not going to happen. Sure, they like to hang out, but don't hold your breath for a sanctified union.

Each, which means every one considered individually, obviously embraces individuality too much to be in a relationship. *Other*, which means different in nature or kind, is a little too unconventional to be married. And George, well, he's handsome, charming, and owns a house on Lake Como—enough said.

Let *each* and *other* (and George and current fling) be who they are: two distinct entities.

They just aren't going to marry *each other*.

Even and *Though*

We probably think *even* and *though* would make a great couple because of the famous adage "opposites attract."

Even is such a dependable word. It means *steady, unchanging*. *Though*, on the other hand, is the opposite. It means *despite the fact that*, which means it is always dealing with varying circumstances. *Though* would be too much drama for *even*. It would be like "The Dude" Lebowski marrying a Real Housewife.

Do you want to be responsible for that union?

***Even though* it would be a disaster, it would be entertaining.**

All and Right

All and *right* are like cousins. It's certainly perfectly acceptable for them NOT to be in a romantic relationship. Accordingly, when *all* and *right* are apart, it means "satisfactory" or "safe."

It's *all right* if you don't marry your cousin.

However, although the majority of states ban marriage between cousins, several states do allow it. Similarly, although the word *alright* is largely considered grammatically incorrect, some people think it should be legal.

But to play it safe, it's still not *all right* to use *alright*.

On-again-off-again: when two words hook up sometimes

These are the words that are constantly breaking up and getting back together. With their constant relationship drama, it's no wonder we get confused.

All and *Together*

All and *together* are like Monica and Chandler before Phoebe caught them kissing: they are in a relationship that they don't want their friends to know about. Therefore, when *all* and *together* are apart it means "in a group":

We are *all together* at the coffee shop again.

All and *together* keep up the charade because when they're together they feel complete. *Altogether* means "completely":

We are *altogether* happy.

All is so fulfilled in the relationship that it doesn't even mind giving up a letter.

All and *Ready*

When *all* and *ready* come together, *all* gives up a letter to form *already*, but *already* is not as fulfilling a union as *altogether*. When *all* and *ready* are together, it's obvious that they have lost that loving feeling—that spark. However, they are so used to each other that when they get lonely they get back together. And then when they're back together, they remember how boring their relationship is and break up again.

Already pretty much means "been there, done that":

Yes, I've *already* heard about the time you scored the winning home run for your Little League team.

When *all* and *ready* break up, they are much more excited. In fact, they are "completely prepared."

They have their eHarmony profiles *all ready* to go.

Every and *Day*

Every and *day* are in the same boat as *all* and *ready*: When *everyday* are together, it is pretty boring. It's an adjective that describes just how *daily*, *ordinary*, or *commonplace* things are:

Our *everyday* life is predictable.
It's nothing to write home about; it's just your *everyday* relationship.

When *every* and *day* break up, life gets a little more exciting. *Every* remains an adjective, but *day* becomes a noun. In this incarnation, *every day* means *each day*. And each day can bring something new:

***Every day* is new and exciting.**
I can date someone new *every day*.

Since it's so much more exciting when they're separated, they definitely spend more time as two words than they do as one.

A and *Part*

A and *part* are that miserable couple you see eating dinner at a restaurant who don't say a word to each other the whole time. Their relationship is so dysfunctional that they feel lonelier when they're together than when they're apart.

Is it any surprise, then, that *apart* means separate:

Even when we're together, I feel like we're *apart*.

I know; it's sad.

And the totally ironic thing about it is that when *a* and *part* are not together they actually feel closer. *A part* means a piece of something that forms a whole:

When they break up, he feels like he's actually still *a part* of her life.

Anyone know a good therapist for these two?

Polygamists: the more the merrier

There's a reality show called *Sister Wives* that documents the life of a polygamist family. This confuses me because I am pretty sure that polygamy is illegal. Therefore, I'm not sure how the family gets away with broadcasting its illegal activity for the world to see without getting arrested. Does this pave the way for reality shows about shoplifters and drug dealers?

Now that I think about it, though, there is another polygamist family out there that has slipped through the cracks: the word *nowadays.*

The word *nowadays* is made up of three words: *now, a,* and *days.*

Probably because polygamy is still technically illegal, many people try to express it as three separate words: *now a days.*

But, it's not three words; it's one big, happily married word:

Maybe *nowadays* polygamy is becoming more acceptable.

Actually, I am pretty sure it is becoming more acceptable because I've recently run into some other three-word marriages: *nonetheless, nevertheless, insofar, whatsoever, and heretofore.*

In that case, I had better start rounding up some brother husbands. Does anyone have Johnny Depp's number?

Exercise 2: How to Choose the Right Relationship

Directions: Underline the form of the word that most accurately depicts the words' relationship.

1. If polygamy is, in fact, becoming more acceptable (nowadays/now a days), would you grab some more spouses?
2. I might get seven spouses so I can have a new one for (everyday/every day) of the week.
3. I wonder if my spouses would get jealous of (eachother/each other).
4. One relationship is (alot/a lot) of work; imagine dealing with seven.
5. At least I would finally be (apart/a part) of a big family.

Quality Control: Words That Don't Make the Grade

Mrs. Robinson, congratulations! All your hard work paid off. I'd also like to extend my congratulations to Stifler's mom and Samantha Jones. Ladies, you're official. Next to the word *cougar* in the dictionary not only will we find "a large, powerful tawny cat"; we will also find "a middle-aged woman seeking a romantic relationship with a younger man."

Every year, new words are added to the dictionary to reflect the vibrant changes in our language and culture. In addition to the vibrant phenomenon of older women desiring the taut, strapping bodies of young men, men are desiring close relationships with one another—only without the sex (BOR-ring!). This paved the way for *bromance* to become an official part of the English lexicon. Congratulations, Han Solo and Chewie, Kirk and Spock, and Matt Damon and Ben Affleck! You're official too.

As you can imagine, it's quite an honor for words to earn a spot in the English language. Consequently, some words have been trying to sneak their way in. But we can't let just any old word in. The new words must add vibrancy to our language. So beware of the following nonvibrant words. Using time-tested tactics, they have fooled many of us into thinking they're the real deal.

Could of, would of, should of

The words *could of, would of,* and *should of* are trying to break into the English language by following in the footsteps of Justin Bieber. When they heard that Bieber was discovered by a talent manager who came across his cover versions of R&B songs on YouTube, they figured that they would break into the English language by doing a cover version of words that already exist.

Here's the thing about cover versions: in order for them to add vibrancy to the existing repertoire, they have to add a unique twist to the original. There's no point if they're just going to sound the same. And that's why I reject *could of, would of,* and *should of.* They sound exactly like the words they are trying to cover: *could have, would have,* and *should have.* (Or if you're in a hurry: *could've, would've,* and *should've.*)

Embracing *could of, would of,* and *should of* as part of the English language is like welcoming a Justin Bieber cover version of a Jonas Brothers song.

Anyways

Anyways is using the same philosophy to make its way into the English language that Norma Jean did when she dyed her brunette locks to platinum blonde and changed her name to Marilyn Monroe: sex sells.

Anyways has tried to slink its way into the English language by taking the word *anyway,* which *is* already a verified word in the English language, and sticking a sexy, curvy, seductive *s* on the end of it.

Many of us have succumbed to its charms, for I have noticed many of us using *anyways* instead of *anyway* in our writing and speech.

However, remember that new words have to add vibrancy to our language, and we already have a ton of words that end in the letter *S*. In fact, *nonetheless* is another word that means *anyway,* and it ends in double S!

Now, that's sexy!

Theirselves

- *Theirselves* is the Eve of our generation. I'm not talking about the woman who sprung from Adam's rib in the Garden of Eden. I'm talking about the Eve from the 1950s Academy Award-winning movie *All About Eve* who (spoiler alert) only pretended to be Margo's biggest fan in order to totally backstab her and take over her role in a Broadway play.
- I don't condone that behavior, and that's why we should definitely keep the word *theirselves* out of our language.
- *Their* is a possessive word (it means belongs to them) and by nature is kind of greedy. So it's no surprise that it's trying to supplant the word *them* in the word *themselves* to get even more stage time in the English language.
- There's absolutely nothing vibrant about backstabbers, so I'd say it's curtains for *theirselves.*

Irregardless

Irregardless thought it could become a hit in the English language if it followed in the footsteps of Sonny and Cher and Hall and Oates. It tried to form a successful duo.

Irregardless took the words *irrespective* and *regardless* and merged them into one. However, *irregardless* is certainly no "I Got You Babe" or "Maneater." It adds absolutely nothing vibrant, and I'll tell you why: it's been done too many times before.

First of all, the two words *irregardless* chose for its duo, *irrespective* and *regardless*, already share the same meaning: without regard for something else. And if that isn't redundant enough, *irregardless* professes to mean the same thing.

Irregardless is showing no regard for the vibrancy of the English language.

EXERCISE 3: CATCH THEM IF YOU CAN

Directions: Identify and circle the word impostors in the following adaptation of the Hans Christian Anderson tale about how to expose a fraud, "The Princess and the Pea."

Once upon a time, a beautiful woman, who claimed to be a princess, sought shelter in a prince's castle on a rainy night. The prince thought she was so hot he would of married her irregardless of whether or not she descended from royalty. The prince's mother, on the other hand, wanted to keep the bloodline pure so her descendants could forever distinguish themselves from mere commoners. So to test the "princess," the queen placed a pea under the twenty mattresses that made up the bed on which the "princess" would sleep. Apparently, real princesses have the sensitivity to feel the pea. In the morning, when asked about her night's sleep, the "princess" said that she would of slept better if it weren't for something hard in the bed. Everyone at the table had to stop theirselves from laughing because she said "something hard in the bed," and they all had dirty minds. Anyways, she went on to show them a pea-size welt on her back, and the prince rejoiced because from now on he was going to be that "something hard in the bed."

4

Missed Periods: Run-on Sentences

One of the most pressing questions of our time is arguably this: Does size matter? Is it about quantity or quality? Is it the size of the boat or the motion of the ocean? Is it the length of the magic wand or the power of the spell?

Obviously, I am referring to sentence size. It's been my experience that we tend to unfairly judge a sentence based on its size rather than its structure. For example, some people see a sentence composed of only a few words and automatically assume that it's not a complete sentence. However, complete sentences can be small if they have the right equipment: a subject, a verb, and a complete thought. For example, here's a sentence with only four words:

The big boat sank.

Subject = Boat

Verb = Sank

Completes a thought = If you went up to someone and said, "The big boat sank," the person may think that it's a weird way to start the conversation, but he or she would understand what happened.

Here's a sentence with only two words:

Boats sink.

It may not be fancy, but it does what it's supposed to do:

Subject = Boats

Verb = Sink

Completes a thought = Boats do sink, right? Ask Kate and Leo.

And if you thought a two-word sentence was exciting, here's a sentence with only one word:

Stop!

I know I said that a sentence must contain at least a subject and a verb, and it looks like this sentence only contains a verb. But when a sentence expresses a command like this one, the subject "you" is assumed. That's right; I'm talkin' to you. (Feel free to read that last sentence using your best *Taxi Driver* De Niro impression.)

So, yes, sentences can bc extremely short and still get the job done. But now we have to contend with people who have the opposite bias: those who think that just because a sentence is long it's a run-on. Technically, a run-on sentence is two sentences run together without the proper punctuation.

First of all, those of us who think we have seen a long sentence probably haven't *really* experienced long. If you want to see a truly long sentence, pick up a copy of James Joyce's novel *Ulysses*, which reportedly contains a 4,391 word sentence. And when you're finished with that one, Jonathan Coe's book *The Rotters Club* contains a sentence made up of 13,955 words.

Hey! Where are you going? Oh, you're just crossing those books off your summer reading list. I don't blame you. I don't suggest actually writing sentences that long. However, my point is that long sentences are not necessarily run-ons. In fact, run-on sentences can even be quite short.

Maybe the confusion stems from the fact that many of us don't really know what a run-on sentence is. We've heard of it, we know it's bad, but what is it really? Allow me to make a short story long. Have you ever been in the middle of something and you're so excited that you don't want to stop because you're afraid that you will lose your mojo, so you just keep on going and going and the next thing you know you miss your period? That, my friends, is how most run-on sentences happen. We forget to insert our periods because we are in such a writing frenzy. A run-on sentence is when we fuse two or more sentences together without using any punctuation to separate them. For example:

I had the strangest dream last night on my couch Johnny Depp was whispering sweet nothings in my ear my mom was telling me to clean my room.

Crazy dream, huh? It's even crazier because that "one" sentence is actually *three* complete sentences that haven't been separated by any punctuation, so we are not quite sure what happened. Was Johnny Depp on my couch whispering sweet nothings in my ear? (Yes, please.)

I had the strangest dream last night. On my couch Johnny Depp was whispering sweet nothings in my ear. My mom was telling me to clean my room.

Or . . .

Was I on my couch, Johnny whispering sweet nothing to the wind, and my mom reciting her famous recipe in my ear? (Mom, I think you left the oven on!)

I had the strangest dream last night on my couch. Johnny Depp was whispering sweet nothings. In my ear my mom was telling me to clean my room.

And remember how I assured you that run-on sentences didn't have to be long? Here's an example of a short one:

I woke up Johnny was gone.

Sentence #1 = I woke up.

Sentence #2 = Johnny was gone.

If we take the proper precautions, though, there's no need for any of us ever to miss our periods. The most effective form of run-on sentence control is to slow down and read our sentences aloud. Let's try it. Read the following group of unpunctuated sentences out loud slowly and insert punctuation where you think it should go:

I had the strangest dream last night I was in my house but it wasn't really *my* house it was a mansion filled with balloons on the couch was this guy wearing a pirate shirt sitting whispering sweet nothings in my ear I looked up to see it was Johnny Depp he told me he wanted me to star in the next *Pirates of the Caribbean* with him he promised that after we finished shooting the movie we would sail away and live happily ever after I was so excited that I would finally have the opportunity to wear my eye patch I packed my suitcase and was about to join Johnny then I heard my mom's voice telling me that I couldn't go anywhere until I did the dishes.

How did it go? When you read slowly, wasn't it clear where one sentence ended and the next one began? Here are all the individual sentences:

1. **I had the strangest dream last night.**
2. **I was in my house but it wasn't really *my* house.**
3. **It was a mansion filled with balloons.**
4. **On the couch was this guy wearing a pirate shirt sitting whispering sweet nothings in my ear.**
5. **I looked up to see it was Johnny Depp.**
6. **He told me he wanted me to star in the next *Pirates of the Caribbean* with him.**

7. **He promised that after we finished shooting the movie we would sail away and live happily ever after.**
8. **I was so excited that I would finally have the opportunity to wear my eye patch.**
9. **I packed my suitcase and was about to join Johnny.**
10. **Then I heard my mom's voice telling me that I couldn't go anywhere until I did the dishes.**

Using this method guarantees a 98 percent success rate of run-on sentence prevention, but there is potentially one negative side effect: the dreaded comma splice.

A comma splice means that a comma has been inserted between two complete sentences. Therefore, if you added any commas to separate the ten sentences in the passage above, you would have committed this all too familiar error.

I get why you'd want to use a comma between some of those sentences. You learned that we use a comma when we pause, and we definitely needed some pauses. And maybe you didn't want to use a period because a period felt like too much of a pause.

Here's the thing: Yes, the comma is related to a pause, but what your English teacher who was too lazy to actually teach you all the comma rules didn't tell you was this valuable bit of information: we don't use a comma *every time* we pause. In this particular case, we can't use a comma because it is against the grammar laws to use a comma between two complete sentences—even small ones. (We'll cover more about commas in the next chapter.)

So we're seemingly in quite a pickle. Sometimes a period provides too much pause between these two sentences, but the comma doesn't provide enough. Luckily, the period and the comma had a drunken one-night stand and produced this adorable little spawn they named the semicolon.

The semicolon, my friends, is the punctuation mark we use to join two complete sentences. When we want to separate two complete sentences, we use the period. When we want to hold them together, we use the semicolon.

Why would we want to hold sentences together? Well, first of all, our sentences might be in a codependent relationship. My fellow codependent readers know what I'm talking about: these sentences depend on one another to complete their meaning. (Apparently, this is okay for sentences but, according to my therapist, not for humans.) Here's an example:

It's bizarre that Will has already started completing Sarah's sentences; they've only been dating for a week.

These two sentences need each other to convey their complete meaning to the reader. It's only bizarre that Will has started completing Sarah's sentences *because* they've only been dating for a week. Usually, it takes . . .

My husband: " . . . one year before couples start completing each other's sentences."

Me: "Hey, I was going to say that. Write your own damn grammar book!"

Here are a couple of other examples of sentences in which the semicolon would be my punctuation mark of choice because they are made up of two sentences that rely on each other to convey the entire meaning:

Sarah never calls Will by his actual name; she calls him Pookie.
If you think that's bad, you should hear his name for her; he calls her Snuggly Wuggly.

In both of these examples, the second sentence builds on the first one to expose the full picture of why we always "have plans" when they invite us out.

We might also want to use a semicolon to hold together two sentences to avoid giving the reader too much time to think about the first sentence before we hit them with the second one. For example, let's say that I was writing an email to my husband explaining why the bank account might not be quite as full as it was earlier in the day. I might include this sentence:

> **I just bought a plane ticket to Cabo; Sharon just went through a divorce and she needs me.**

Since I hit my husband with Sharon's divorce in the same sentence as Cabo, there's simply no way he could get mad!

But beware: once we discover the semicolon's unique power, we tend to want to use it all the time. Use the semicolon like you would use any powerful weapon (your best pick-up line or your most effective push-up bra): carefully and sparingly.

EXERCISE 4: OH, HOW YOU DO RUN-ON!

Directions: Unleash your semicolons and periods and fix the run-ons in the following passage.

I had the strangest dream last night I was in my house but it wasn't really *my* house it was a mansion filled with balloons on the couch was this guy wearing a pirate shirt sitting whispering sweet nothings in my ear I looked up to see it was Johnny Depp he told me he wanted me to star in the next *Pirates of the Caribbean* with him he promised that after we finished shooting the movie we would sail away and live happily ever after I was so excited that I would finally have the opportunity to wear my eye patch I packed my suitcase and was about to join Johnny then I heard my mom's voice telling me that I couldn't go anywhere until I did the dishes.

5

More Than a Feeling: Commas

Does this sound familiar to anyone: "It just feels so right"? This is what you kept telling your skeptical best friend when she warned you not to go out with him. (You know which *him* I'm talking about.) Next thing you know, it's two weeks later, and you are curled up on the couch watching *Love Actually*, your tears adding a strangely delicious saltiness to the half-devoured tub of double chocolate fudge ice cream you are clutching. Now you are crying to your best friend, "I don't get it. It just *felt* so right!"

This is why we need rules, my friends. Here are a few: Never date your friend's ex. Never date anyone who isn't devastated that *Arrested Development* was cancelled. Never date a guy (or, for that matter, a girl) whose nickname is Big Daddy. Never date anyone who says *chillax.* And, ladies, never date a guy who wears a mock turtleneck. (Okay, that last one is just a personal pet peeve, but the other ones are undebatable.)

It's equally important to follow our heads rather than our hearts when dealing with commas. When I question my students about their comma placement, most of them tell me they insert the comma when they "feel like it should be there." When they *feel* like it should be there! Is it just me, or is it weird that my students have some kind of emotional connection with a mark of punctuation?

The fact that they have feelings about commas is not just bizarre; it's dangerous. It's dangerous because we don't all feel the same way about the comma: most of us either love it or we hate it. Those of us who hate commas tend to just say screw it and leave them out completely. This is okay if we don't mind being responsible for our readers passing out from breath deprivation at the end of our sentences. Those of us who love commas tend to put them EVERYWHERE. Comma lovers need to be very careful: after a long sentence, you may get sued for whiplash.

Forget about how you *feel* about the comma. I know it's small and cute and curvy, but we've got to harden our hearts and use our heads. Instead of letting our emotions dictate our comma placement, why not follow these good old-fashioned rules:

Commas for Clarity

After we've been dumped, many of us can't seem to move on until we get closure. We just have to make sure (for the tenth time) that he or she fully realizes what a gigantic mistake it was to break up with us. Basically, we just want to have clarity before we move on to the next relationship.

With such an appreciation for closure, it is no wonder that we are all pretty good about inserting a comma to separate items in a series—you know, to make it clear when one item has ended so another can begin. If we didn't insert the commas when we listed three or more items, it would be hard to tell where one item ended and the next began. For example, Jack doesn't quite understand why Kim broke up with him, so he asked his friend Bill the following:

> **Do you think it was due to my pet python escaping daily requesting threesomes with her friends Laura and Samantha texting constantly while Kim and I were on dates or forgetting her birthday three years in a row?**

Well, it's going to be difficult for Bill to provide Jack with an accurate answer if Jack doesn't insert the commas. Bill won't know if Jack's python escaped daily and Jack requested threesomes specifically with Laura and Samantha:

Do you think it was due to my pet python escaping daily, requesting threesomes with her friends Laura and Samantha, texting constantly while Kim and I were on dates, or forgetting her birthday three years in a row?

Or if the python escaped once, Jack requested threesomes daily, and it was Laura and Samantha who texted him constantly:

Do you think it was due to my pet python escaping, daily requesting threesomes with her friends, Laura and Samantha texting constantly while Kim and I were on dates, or forgetting her birthday three years in a row?

But, as I said before, most of us remember these commas. We are really good at inserting the commas to separate items in a series. Here are a couple more examples:

Kim said she broke up with Jack because he was immature, arrogant, and bad in bed.

Item #1 Item #2

Item #3

She felt great after burning his favorite t-shirt, smashing his Xbox, and calling his mother.

Item #1 Item #2

Item #3

One mistake we tend to make is that sometimes we require too much closure. It's kind of like your friend who just can't quite accept that her ex has moved on. He could be making out with his new girlfriend right in front of her and your friend still insists that they "need to talk." Well, sometimes we do the same thing with commas. We use them for closure, but there's closure enough already. This happens when the word *and* is involved. When we join our items with the word *and*, we don't need a comma because the *and* clearly separates our items.

Here's an example of this error:

Brad unfriended Jennifer on Facebook, and changed his phone number.

We have two items:

Item #1 – unfriended Jennifer on Facebook
Item #2 – changed his phone number

However, the *and* already separates the first item from the second, so using the comma is unnecessary. The *and* makes it abundantly clear that the first item has ended. This is the correct form of the sentence:

Brad unfriended Jennifer on Facebook and changed his phone number.

But, wait! I forgot something. He did something else. He also adopted several children with a woman he just met. The new sentence is:

Brad unfriended Jennifer on Facebook and changed his phone number and adopted several children with a woman he just met.

And, again, since the *ands* make it clear where one item ends and the next begins, we don't need commas.

What's that you say? You want to know why I would use all of those *ands* when I could just insert a comma between those items. Well, I agree with you. Although the sentence above is "technically" correct, I like your idea. It sounds better without all of the *ands*. Let's make this our new sentence:

Brad unfriended Jennifer on Facebook, changed his phone number, and adopted several children with a woman he just met.

Now, many of you may be thinking that this comma makes sense; it's separating items in a series.

Brad unfriended Jennifer on Facebook, changed his phone number, and adopted several children with a woman he just met.

But you are wondering why we would put a comma here if the *and* "supposedly" provides enough closure.

Well, it's like cream in your coffee, tonic in your vodka, or toys in your bedroom; it's up to you whether you want to add it or not. If you feel like adding a comma before the *and* separating the second to last and last item in a series, go for it. If you don't, that's cool too. Just be consistent.

Remember, though, the optional comma before *and* only applies when it is separating items in a series of three or more. It's called "the serial comma." There are going to be times when we *have to* put a comma before *and*, and there will also be times when, even if we really, really feel like it, we can't put a comma before *and*.

As shown above, we can't put a comma before *and* when it is separating only two items. However, we must put a comma before *and* when it joins two complete sentences. For example:

Jennifer will bounce back because she has good friends, and she also has good hair.

Complete sentence — Comma — Complete sentence

However, if there is not a complete sentence on EACH side of the *and*, it is incorrect to add a comma. For example:

Jennifer will bounce back because she had good friends and good hair.

Complete sentence — No comma — **Not** a complete sentence

Exercise 5A: Breaking Up Is Hard to Do

Directions: Break up the following sentences by inserting a comma before *and* when it's required:

1. Lloyd Dobler was desperate to win back Diane Court and blasted a Peter Gabriel love song outside her bedroom window.
2. Alexandra did not cope well with being jilted by Dan and she boiled his daughter's bunny.
3. Rhett told Scarlett that he didn't give a damn and walked out the door.
4. Joel couldn't cope with his breakup and had every memory from the relationship erased from his mind.
5. Jack Berger didn't want to date Carrie Bradshaw anymore, and he communicated this to her on a Post-it note.

Let's Do It for the BOYS

We just talked about how we must add a comma before *and* if the *and* joins two complete sentences. Well, *and* is not alone. It belongs to an exclusive group of which there are six other members. That's right: there are six other words like *and* that require a comma before them if there is a complete sentence on each side of them. This group is called the FANBOYS.

When I think of FANBOYS, I would like to imagine that they are a group of seven boys who, while I sun myself poolside, fan me with palm leaves and attend to my every need, but it's really just an acronym to help us remember these little words:

For	**Or**
And	**Yet**
Nor	**So**
But	

When we see one of these seven words in a sentence, we insert a comma before it **if—and only if**—there is a complete sentence on each side of it. Here are a few examples:

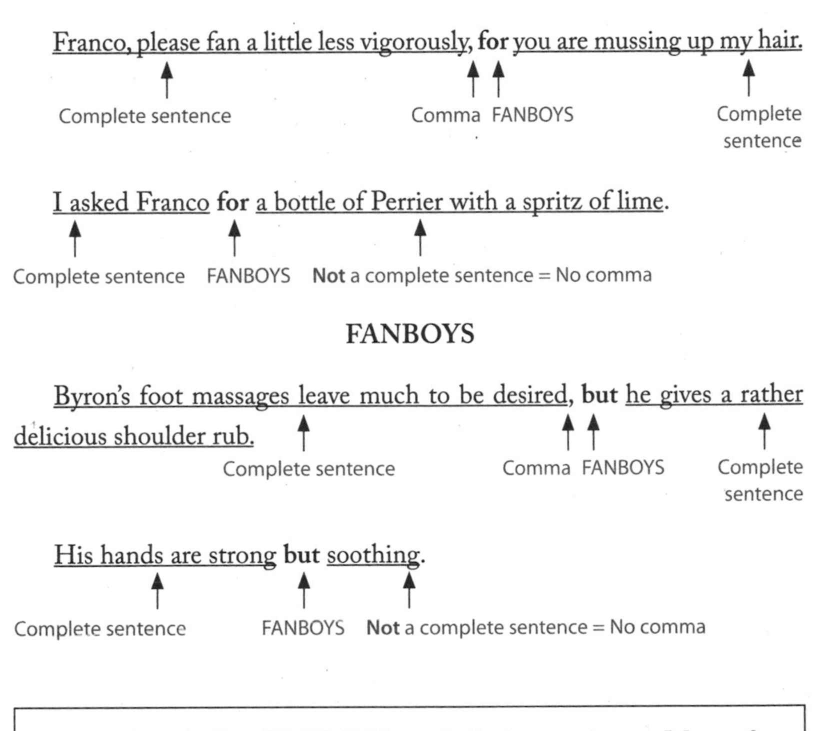

*Remember: the B in FANBOYS stands for *but*, not *because*. Many of us like to insert a comma before *because*, but 98 percent of the time we don't. (I don't care what your fifth grade teacher told you. He was wrong!)

FANBOYS

In the next example, there is a complete sentence on both sides of *so*, but we don't insert a comma when *so* is short for *so that*:

I must be refreshed hourly by the juice of ten plump grapes **so** (that) I can sun a little longer.

Although all the BOYS didn't come out to play (I sent them to the gym to work on their pecs and abs), I hope you get the idea. Memorize this list of words:

For
And
Nor
But
Or
Yet
So

And you know what to do: when you see one of these little fellows in a sentence, stop, look both ways, see if there's a complete sentence on each side. If there is, insert a comma; if there's not, keep on walking.

Exercise 5b: The Other Kind of FANBOYS

Directions: When appropriate, insert commas before the FANBOYS in the following sentences about the kind of fanboy I dated in high school.

1. I felt like I would never be good enough for him for it's impossible to compete with Princess Leia in the golden bikini.
2. We would have gone to the prom but the big comic book convention was on the same weekend.
3. He kept all of his Star Wars action figures in their original packaging so he could sell them for millions of dollars one day.
4. He tried to learn to speak Vulcan but never quite mastered it.
5. He wanted his ears to look like Spock's so he slept with clothespins on the tips of his ears for a year.

Commas Because There's Never a Second Chance to Make a First Impression

First impressions stick. That's why it's so important that we do tedious things like remember to wear deodorant, brush our teeth, and insert commas in the correct places. I mean, imagine what you would think of me if these were the first sentences of mine that you met:

When I eat my sister always picks off my plate.
If you're ever in the mood to give head over to the local charity.

Admit it: after reading the sentences, your first impression was that I am some kind of sicko. Maybe after a couple of reads, you realized that I'm neither a cannibal nor a pervert, but for the rest of our lives, if someone mentions *Missed Periods and Other Grammar Scares*, you'll say, "Oh yeah, that's the book written by that perverted chick who eats people." Geez. Tough crowd. If I had only put those commas:

When I eat, my sister always picks off my plate.
If you're ever in the mood to give, head over to the local charity.

To avoid those unfortunate misunderstandings for which we are judged forevermore, allow me to explain this comma rule. The rule applies when we have a very special type of sentence: one that is comprised of two parts: an **introductory phrase** and a **complete sentence.**

The **complete sentence** is the main attraction of the sentence. The **introductory phrase**, on the other hand, is the part of the sentence that is like the emcee: it sets the stage for the main attraction. It tells us readers a little something about the independent clause to whet our appetites. The **introductory phrase** "introduces" **when, where, why,** or **under what circumstances** the **independent clause** takes place. We need to insert a comma between the **introductory phrase** and an **independent clause.**

So here's the big question: How do we know when we have an introductory phrase? Well, I'm glad you asked. A good indication is that our sentence starts with one of these *when, where, why, or under what circumstances* words or phrases:

When	Where	Why	Under What Circumstances
As soon as	Above	Because	As long as
After	Across	In order to	Although
At	Behind	So that	By
Before	Below	To	Despite
During	Beneath		Even though
When	Beside		If
Whenever	In		Provided that
While	On		Since
	Under		Unless
			With

Don't be shy; have another look at those words and phrases. Which ones do you start your sentences with? Some of the more popular choices are *if, because, although, in, when,* and *since*, but they're all fair game. If we start our sentences with one of these words, there is a 90% chance our sentence will require a comma. We just need to make sure we have both ingredients: an introductory phrase followed by an independent clause. Here are some examples of such sentences. See what a difference a comma can make:

- Without the comma:

Before you begin turning a trick is to find a spot on which to focus.

- With the comma:

<u>*Before* you begin turning</u>, <u>a trick is to find a spot on which to focus.</u>

↑ Key word; *when* introductory phrase

↑ complete sentence

- Without the comma:

Behind the portrait of the family jewels that belonged to your grandmother are hidden.

- With the comma:

Behind **the portrait of the family, jewels that belonged to your grandmother are hidden.**

Key word; *Where* introductory phrase complete sentence

- Without the comma:

Because Kate loves to sleep around 50 percent of her day was spent looking for pillows.

- With the comma:

Because **Kate loves to sleep, around 50 percent of her day was spent looking for pillows.**

Key word; *Why* introductory phrase complete sentence

- Without the comma:

If I had to pick my nose would be the first to go under the knife.

- With the comma:

If **I had to pick, my nose would be the first to go under the knife.**

Key word; *Under what circumstances* phrase complete sentence

There are, however, those rare occasions when one of those key words begins our sentence yet we don't need a comma. It will look like you have an introductory phrase, but there won't be a complete sentence following it. Let's go through the process together to determine whether or not the following sentence requires a comma:

Behind the portrait of the family are grandmother's jewels.

The sentence starts with the word *Behind*, so our radar goes off. We start to get all hot and bothered because we think we may have an introductory phrase on our hands. "Where are we going to put that comma?" we ask ourselves. In other words, where does that introductory phrase end?

1. Just as we are poised to stick that cute little comma after *family*—because that's where the *where* phrase ends—we remember to stop and ask ourselves, "Is there a complete sentence following the comma?" In other words, can "are grandmother's jewels" stand alone as a complete thought?
2. We decide to try it. We turn to the person sitting next to us in the bus and say, "Are grandmother's jewels."
3. The person looks at us like we are crazy and then gets up to sit somewhere else. Apparently, "are grandmother's jewels" doesn't make sense on its own.
4. We put the comma away.

Exercise 5c: Make a Good Impression

Directions: Create sentences that begin with the word provided. Don't forget the commas!

Example: **To** make a good impression at my job interview, I decided not to mention anything about the time I got so mad at a photocopy machine that I beat it up.

1. **If** ______________________________
2. **When** ______________________________
3. **Because** ______________________________
4. **Since** ______________________________
5. **With** ______________________________

Commas to Set Details Apart, and Yes, I Do Need All Those Jeans

My jeans collection is a constant source of contention between my husband and me. About once a week, he'll gaze at the mountain of jeans folded on the closet shelves, shake his head, and ask me, "Do you really *need* all of those jeans?"

"OF COURSE I NEED ALL OF THEM! What am I supposed to do? Wear my boots over these wide-legged jeans? Do you expect me to wear these light denim jeans in the winter? And what about these skinny jeans? How am I going to fit into them when I'm bloated? Hey! Where are you going? Get back here! I haven't even gotten around to the issue of high-waisted versus low-waisted."

Well, it looks like he's gone. Good. Now, I can tell you the truth: I don't really *need* ALL of my pairs of jeans. I do have two identical pairs of Seven jeans, but I couldn't help it: I bought the second pair because they were only $40 at T.J.Maxx. Forty bucks for Sevens! You can't pass that up. And I do have a pair of Gap jeans from the '90s that I will probably never wear again, but they are my weight control jeans: when they fit, I'm good, but when they're snug, it means I have to lay off the Haagen-Dazs for a week or so.

This issue of needs versus wants also comes up when we are writing sentences. Sometimes we need every single word in our sentence, and sometimes, although we don't need certain words, we want them.

To explain what I mean, let's think about a sentence's purpose. Why do sentences exist? Sentences exist to convey information to a reader, right? For example, I'd like everyone to know this:

My Gap jeans from the '90s fit perfectly this morning.

Every word in that sentence is needed to convey my meaning. There are words I could take away and the sentence would still make sense, but meaning would be lost. For example, I could take away "from the '90s" and "perfectly" and "this morning" and still have a complete sentence:

My Gap jeans fit.

However, it's crucial that my readers understand that I am talking about my Gap jeans from the '90s because those are the ones I use as my weight barometer. It's also important that I get across to my readers that they fit me "perfectly." There's a big difference between being able to squeeze into them and having them glide right on. And it's also important that my readers know that they fit perfectly "this morning" because I am trying to show off about my present situation.

Now, let's say I want to give you some added detail about these Gap jeans; however, the added detail is not really needed to communicate the main idea of my sentence. Well, that's fine; I can do that. I just need to make sure I put commas around the extra information:

My Gap jeans from the '90s, which I wore on my first date with Jake Miller, fit perfectly this morning.

The fact that I wore the jeans on my first date with Jake is just extra information. It has nothing to do with identifying which jeans I wore or how they fit, which is the main point of my sentence. It's just a little something I wanted you to know because:

Jake Miller was the most popular guy in high school.

And he asked ME out on a date! I know, right? Again, I need every word in this sentence. He wasn't just popular; he was THE MOST POPULAR. However, there is a little extra something you should know about Jake, especially if you are thinking about going out with him:

Jake Miller, who kisses like he's giving CPR, was the most popular guy in school.

"Who kisses like he's giving CPR" is extra information. It has nothing to do with Jake's high school popularity status, which is the main point of the sentence. So, as you can see, I had to enclose it in commas.

On the other hand, in the following sentence, "who kiss like they're giving CPR" is not extra information because without it meaning would be lost from the sentence:

Guys who kiss like they're giving CPR should have to attend kissing classes.

If I take out "who kiss like they're giving CPR," this is my sentence:

Guys should have to attend kissing classes.

However, I am not suggesting that ALL guys should have to attend kissing classes, only the ones who kiss like they're giving CPR. Therefore, it's essential information, not extra information, so it does not require commas.

(But, now that I think about it, all guys should have to attend kissing classes. It couldn't hurt.)

Exercise 5D: Did You Really Need to Tell Me That?

Directions: The person who wrote the following sentences is a VERY open person. All of the sentences share personal information; in some sentences the information is necessary while in others it's extra. Insert commas in the following sentences to set apart the extra information.

1. Richard who has three nipples just got hired at my work.
2. The dress I let you borrow to wear on your date the one I wore when I made out with Steve in the back of the car needs to be dry-cleaned.

3. I'd like to introduce you to the nice girl who held my hair for me when I vomited at the club the other night.
4. I have a thing for men who have outie belly buttons.
5. Eddie's stand-up comedy routine last night which made me laugh so hard I peed a little bit in my pants was his best one yet.

I hope you have learned to control your feelings about the comma. When it comes to matters of the comma, don't follow your heart—follow the rules.

6

I Do: Apostrophes

Marriage is great. You no longer have to agonize over finding a date for weddings. You get tax breaks. And assuming everyone sticks to their vows, you don't have to worry about contracting herpes. But there are sacrifices that must be made. Big ones. My closet space, for example, has been chopped in half. I have to sneak shoe purchases into the house in Trader Joe's bags. I can't spend an entire Saturday sacked out on the couch watching *Real Housewives* marathons because SOMEBODY can't stand more than two hours of "listening to all of those whiney voices." Maybe that's what the wedding ring is really all about: compensation for these sacrifices we make when we become a union.

People, by the way, are not the only independent entities that sacrifice in order to "become one." Words do too. When *do* and *not* united to form *don't, not* sacrificed its *o*. *Will* gave up its *wi* when it united with *he* to form *he'll.* And when *I* and *am* tied the knot and formed *I'm, am* relinquished its *a*. And for those sacrifices, these married words, which are called contractions, get an apostrophe where those letters once were, making the apostrophe the punctuation equivalent of the wedding ring.

There is, however, a troubling trend emerging. Words aren't wearing their apostrophes like they used to. I don't know if they're trying to pick up on other words or what, but when certain married words neglect to wear their apostrophes, they might be mistaken for their single friends:

The identity of **he'll** just went to **hell.**

She'll is like a **shell** of its former self.

We'll looks like it wishes it were a **well.**

I'll looks like it is **ill.**

And, **we're** looks like it **were** not itself.

I, for one, know that I don't want to be mistaken for my nonmarried friends. You know how they are: always out partying and going to Cabo for the weekend and spending their disposable income on new shoes and expensive meals. Hey! Wait a sec . . .

Technology is partly to blame for today's missing apostrophe epidemic. For some reason, proper punctuation is not on the forefront of our minds when we are commenting on our high school sweetheart's newly broad-casted single status on Facebook. I also blame sexting. (Sexting is short for sloppy texting, right?) We simply can't be bothered to add an apostrophe while simultaneously text messaging and trying to get over from the fast lane to the freeway exit in a quarter of a mile.

Those of us with an iPhone may be feeling smug right now because our phone adds our apostrophes for us when we text message. I'm sure the iPhone means well, but like a mother who cooks and cleans for her son who's forty years old and doesn't know how to boil water, your iPhone is just an enabler. And, might I add, not always correct. The other day I was texting the word *its*, and my iPhone incorrectly changed it to *it's*. Now, I'm thinking about changing to the Droid.

Another way the apostrophe is like the wedding ring is that it also symbolizes possession. Stop looking at me like that; you know it kind of does. When we see a cute guy or girl with that band encircling the ring finger on their left hand, we don't think to ourselves, "That ring symbolizes that person's eternal love and devotion"; we think, "Damn, that person is taken!"

Possession is tricky. It brings up issues of jealousy, codependence, self-esteem, and incorrect apostrophe placement. Dr. Phil can help you with the psychological stuff, but I can provide you with some valuable insight into how to use apostrophes to show possession:

Rule #1:

If only **one person or thing is doing the possessing,** most of the time we ***add 's*** to the end of the word.

To demonstrate this rule, let's take a look at Kevin and Jane. It has been a week since they arrived home from their honeymoon in Bora Bora; this is what has been going on:

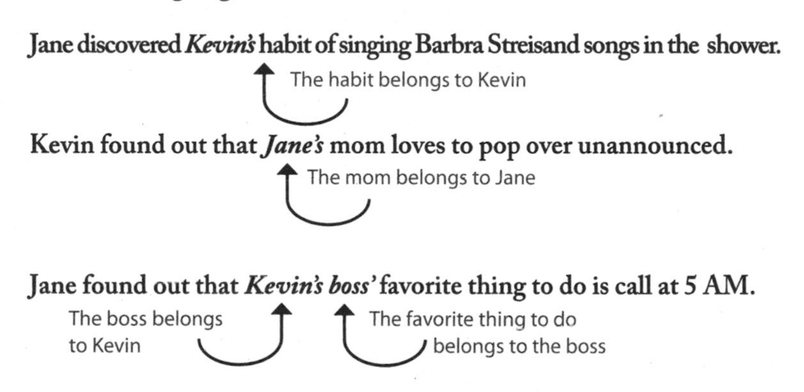

Note: Look at the word *boss* in the sentence above. Even though we are only talking about one boss, when a singular word that is possessive ends in *s* already, we have the option of whether or not to add an *s* after the apostrophe. We can if we want to, but if *boss's* seems like *S* overkill, we can just leave it off. It's our choice.

Rule #2:

If **more than one person or thing is doing the owning,** most of the time we ***add an apostrophe after the S.***

To demonstrate this rule, let's fast-forward to a few months after the honeymoon. It looks like Kevin and Jane had a great time because they're already having their first child— and they're totally freaking out.

First of all, they're afraid they will duplicate their *parents'* mistakes.
The mistakes belong to four people, so we put the apostrophe after the *s*.

If we put the apostrophe before the S, it would mean that the mistakes belong to only one parent, which is obviously not fair to that parent. It would also mean that Kevin and Jane share a parent (because the sentence would read *their parent's mistakes),* which would make the fact that they are having a child together illegal and pretty gross.

Rule #3

When **more than one IRREGULAR person or thing** is doing the possessing, **the apostrophe goes before the *S*.**

When we are indicating that there is more than one of something, the **REGULAR** thing to do is slap an *s* on the end of the word, like this:

One (Singular)	More than one (Plural)
parent	parents
sleepless night	sleepless nights
tantrum	tantrums
stretch mark	stretch marks

However, there are some irregular words that change in a different way when they go from singular to plural, like these:

Singular	Plural
man	men
woman	women
child	children

Don't ask me why the people who invented the English language wanted to complicate everything and didn't just slap an *s* on the end of man to make it plural (they must be the ancestors of the people who decided that one TV required three remote controls). But, as a result, we don't have *a few good mans*; we have *a few good men*. And we don't have *two beautiful childs*; we have *two beautiful children*.

And, when one of these irregular plural words is possessive, unlike the regular ones, the apostrophe goes before the *S*.

Let's look at these two sentences:

1. **The doctor said it is the man's responsibility not to pass out during childbirth.**

Singular Possessive

Or

2. **The doctor said it is men's responsibility not to pass out during childbirth.**

Plural Possessive

Both of these sentences are correct.

Now, we can understand why sentence 1 is correct (because the responsibility belongs to one man so we add an 's). But, sentence 2 is plural, so shouldn't the apostrophe go after the *S*?

In order to understand how all this works, we need to back up. The reason the placement of the apostrophe is of the utmost importance is because it lets the reader know whether one or more than one person or thing is doing the possessing. For example:

Singular Possessive

1. **Kevin and Jane thought the *doctor's* advice to rub Jane's stomach with orange marmalade for the last three months was strange.**

Or

Plural Possessive

2. **Kevin and Jane thought the *doctors'* advice to rub Jane's stomach with orange marmalade for the last three months was strange.**

Due to the placement of the apostrophe, Sentence 1 indicates that only one doctor gave that advice while Sentence 2 indicated that more than one doctor gave that advice. Now, this is an important distinction because if only one doctor said it, they could probably assume that he is a little crazy and save their marmalade for their scones, but if it was a consensus, well, it looks like they'll be taking a trip to Costco.

But when we make *man* plural, it becomes *men*, and because the spelling changes, we don't depend on the placement of the apostrophe to indicate whether we mean one or more than one. Therefore, when men, women, and children possess something, we simply add the *'s* to the end:

In an article, Jane read that *men's* fear of the *women's* attention shifting to focus on the *children's* needs results in the men reverting back to childhood.

And she believed it when she saw Kevin sucking his thumb.

I have bad news for you: it didn't work out between Jane and Kevin. Jane simply couldn't handle Kevin's Barbra Streisand obsession, and Kevin couldn't deal with Jane's mother's daily visits. But the split was amicable, and they agreed to share joint custody of their child. And speaking of joint custody, that brings us to rule #4:

Rule #4

When we express joint custody, only the last-named member gets the *'s*. However, if we are indicating separate ownership, both names get the *'s*:

Joint ownership: Jane and Kevin*'s* daughter, Barbara, turned out to be a well-adjusted kid.

(The daughter belongs to both Jane and Kevin.)

Separate ownership: Jane*'s* and Kevin*'s* *hearts* eventually mended, so they started to date other people.

(Kevin and Jane don't share a heart. It's biologically impossible.)

When we are craving a relationship, we start contemplating whether the most random people—like the person in front of us in line at Starbucks or the one stopped next to us at the stop light—are "the one," right? That's exactly what Jane and Kevin went through. In such a delicate state, it's hard not to feel lonely, but we must maintain our standards.

We also have to remember to maintain our standards when we use apostrophes. What tends to happen after we learn about apostrophes is that we freak out and want to bestow an apostrophe on every word that ends in an *S*. We have to remember: not every word that ends in an *S* gets an apostrophe—only the possessive ones. Most words that end in *S* are just plural and don't require an apostrophe. For example:

After the split-up, both Kevin and Jane went on a couple of *dates* from hell.

No apostrophe because nothing belongs to *dates*.

One of the *ladies* Kevin took to dinner talked about her ex-boyfriend the whole time.

No apostrophe because nothing belongs to *ladies*.

One of Jane's *date's* two front teeth was missing because his ex-girlfriend knocked it out.

This one gets an apostrophe because the two front teeth belong (well . . . belonged) to the date.

Basically, apostrophes are like our affections—we should definitely bestow them, but we don't want to go around sticking them everywhere. We wouldn't want to get a reputation or anything.

Exercise 6: Have Some Self-Respect

Directions: For numbers 1-3, insert apostrophes in the sentences only when they're required. Don't go sticking them in front of every *S* you see. For 4-5, choose the correct answer.

1. Jane went on a blind date with her coworkers brother Sam, who took her to meet his parents on their first date.
2. During Kevins first date with Alicia, she talked about her last three ex-boyfriends penis size.
3. Lola seemed great, but Kevin got suspicious when he saw her walk into the mens bathroom.
4. ________________ dating experiences were equally disastrous.
   A. Kevin's and Jane
   B. Kevin's and Jane's
   C. Kevin and Jane's
5. They both decided to revise their ______________ on eHarmony.
   A. profiles
   B. profile's
   C. profiles'

7

Drumroll, Please: Colons

If I could change one thing about myself, what would it be? Well, that's an interesting question. I could certainly go for some longer legs. Increasing a cup-size would be nice. I've always kind of wanted green eyes and longer eyelashes and a flawless complexion and . . . Wait a minute! I should be ashamed of myself. All of these changes are so superficial. If I could change one thing about myself, I'd change something on the inside. I would remove the part of my brain that can't help but associate Richard Gere with gerbils.

For those of you who don't know what I'm talking about, several years ago, there was a rumor . . .

You know what? Never mind. I am not going to tarnish your Richard Gere experience. I don't want you going through life afraid that if you do run into Mr. Gere you'll make an embarrassing Freudian slip and say something like, "You were great in *An Officer and a Gerbilman.*"

And it's not just that. Richard Gere deserves much more than such a paltry association. We're talking about a man who has played one of the most important roles in film history: the role of a man who gave his credit card to a woman to shop Rodeo Drive—with no spending limit. Did you hear me? No spending limit! And he's done some almost-as-commendable things off the screen too, such as promote world peace and raise AIDS awareness. He deserves more than being known as the gerbil guy.

When I think about Richard Gere, I can't help but simultaneously think about the colon. This poor punctuation mark is also unfairly pigeonholed. When most of us think of the colon, we think list. More specifically, we think that a colon's sole function is to introduce a list. Well, there are a couple of things wrong with that association. First of all, a colon does not introduce every single list. Second of all, a colon is so much more than a list introducer. In fact, the colon is arguably one of the most exciting punctuation marks out there. If we are going to associate the colon with anything, it should be with a drumroll.

Just like a drumroll builds anticipation, so does the colon.

Here's an example:

The craziest thing happened.

Drumroll . . .

I was picked up by a hot guy driving a sports car that cornered like it was on rails.

Since it's not possible to write a drumroll, we use the colon:

The craziest thing happened: I was picked up by a hot guy driving a sports car that cornered like it was on rails.

Because the colon is so dang exciting, it has one condition: it demands to be placed only after a complete sentence.

Correct: **There is one thing I absolutely hate: when strawberry seeds get stuck in my teeth.** Complete sentence

Incorrect: **I absolutely hate it when: strawberry seeds get stuck in my teeth.** Not a complete sentence

Correct: **I absolutely hate it when strawberry seeds get stuck in my teeth.**

If the colon is all about building anticipation and calling attention to what follows it, how did it get its association with the list? I can only imagine it's because there are certain lists to which we want to call attention.

I have three rules: never let a man see you floss, always listen to Prince while bathing, and never kiss on the lips.

Complete sentence

One of the most common colon-related mistakes we make, however, is inserting the colon before a list that isn't introduced by a complete sentence. Here are some examples:

My favorite outfit used to be: a blonde wig, thigh-high boots, and a minidress with the sides cut out.

The saleswomen on Rodeo Drive made a big mistake—a HUGE one—because my new wardrobe includes expensive items such as: a black lace dress, a gorgeous red gown, and a brown polka-dotted dress.

So we know that a colon is preceded by a complete sentence, but as you can see, it doesn't necessarily have to be followed by one. When the information following the colon is not a complete sentence, we don't capitalize the word directly following the colon:

I have the best idea: a *Pretty Woman* sequel.

We only capitalize it if it's a word that normally requires capitalization. (See Chapter 11 for capitalization rules.)

I have the best idea: *Pretty Woman 2: Vivian Takes Rodeo Drive*

Pretty is capitalized only because we capitalize movie titles.

When the information following the colon is one complete sentence, we have the option of whether or not to capitalize it:

Here's the premise: She opens a sex shop next door to the boutique on Rodeo Drive that snubbed her.

Or

Here's the premise: she opens a sex shop next door to the boutique on Rodeo Drive that snubbed her.

However, if the information following the colon is two or more complete sentences, we must capitalize the first word after the colon:

Of course, there will be a happy ending: The snobby boutique women eventually loosen up and become Vivian's best customers. Also, Kit, Vivian's spunky prostitute friend from the original, marries one of Edward's rich friends.

And if you needed further proof as to why it's a travesty to limit the colon's identity to preceding lists, allow me to introduce some more wonderful things that the colon does.

It separates hours from minutes:

I met him on the corner of Hollywood and Vine at 3:05 AM.

It follows a formal business letter greeting:

Dear Mr. Lewis:

(A formal greeting is Dear + Mr. or Ms. + the last name. An informal greeting is Hello + first or last name and is followed by a comma.)

And it has one secret talent:

It can lie on its back and disguise itself as two periods. (The other punctuation marks think it's hilarious!)

EXERCISE 7: RENAISSANCE MEN

Directions: Richard Gere and the colon aren't the only men who have been unfairly pigeonholed. The following sentences give these men credit where credit is due. Add colons where needed.

1. Einstein did more than discover the theory of relativity. Even though he was married to Elsa, he also did Estella, Ethel, Toni, and his "Russian spy lover," Margarita.
2. Daniel Radcliffe will probably always be known as the guy who played Harry Potter, but I will remember him for a different role the one in the play Equus in which he played a naked stable boy who had an obsession with horses.
3. Bill Clinton will go down in history for not having sexual relations with Monica Lewinsky, but he also accomplished other important feats he was the governor of Arkansas and the 42nd president of the United States.
4. To me, Ozzy Osbourne will always be the guy who bit the head off a bat, but he seems to have a softer side since his favorite TV shows as a child were reportedly *I Love Lucy*, *Lassie*, and *Roy Rogers*.
5. And here's one final Richard Gere fact he was also a phenomenal gymnast.

8

Goldilocks and the Three Bars: En Dashes, Em Dashes, and Hyphens

I know that in Chapter 4 I argued that size doesn't matter, but I don't know what I was thinking. There are some ladies to whom size matters a lot. One such lady that comes to mind is Goldilocks—that girl wouldn't even deign to sit in a chair lest it was the perfect size. (She was also quite particular about firmness, but that's another story.)

Let's say Goldilocks came across these three varying sizes of horizontal bars:

Which size do you think would be "just right" for her?

Judging from how picky Goldi was about which bed she slept in, I assume she's not afraid to demand comfort, so I am pretty sure she wouldn't choose the second bar. The second bar is called an *en dash*, and it's the least comfortable of the three. There is no key on a computer keyboard for an en dash, so in order to create it, we have to engage in a complicated key combination. (For PC users, it's *Ctrl Num and* -, and for Mac users it's *option hyphen.)*

We use the en dash when we want to express a range of values:

Goldilocks will only sleep on Egyptian cotton sheets with a *300–400* thread count.

She only eats porridge that is 98–100 degrees.

Goldilocks might choose the third bar, which is known as the *em dash*. The reason I think she might prefer that one is because it's a lot like her: it loves a dramatic entrance and plops itself down wherever it damn well pleases.

Like an exclamation point, the em dash may be used to provide emphasis, but the exclamation point must go at the end of a sentence—the em dash can go anywhere:

There's a little blonde girl—in my bed.

None of my porridge—not even one little drop—is left.

In order to create the em dash, we type the minus sign twice on our keyboard, and then it magically merges together. But two keystrokes might even be too much work for a girl who's so lazy she won't even make her own porridge (even though nowadays all you have to do is add water). So maybe Goldilocks would choose the first bar. The first bar is called a hyphen, which requires we keystroke the minus sign only once.

So when do we use a hyphen? That's the million dollar question. Or is it the million-dollar question? We use the hyphen to link words, but how do we know which words we are supposed to link?

It's confusing. Sometimes we hyphenate words:

Goldilocks was a *fair-haired* young girl.

Sometimes we keep them as separate words:

Goldilocks had *fair hair*.

And sometimes we combine two words into one word:

Goldilocks treated the three bears' house like it was her own personal *fairground*.

There is not an all-encompassing rule that dictates when to hyphenate words. The general consensus is that if we want to know if a word is hyphenated we should check the dictionary. However, it is also the general consensus that words should be hyphenated when the hyphen helps clarify meaning. For example, the meaning of the following sentences changes depending on whether or not the words are hyphenated:

Goldilocks was not a dirty-blonde.
Goldilocks was not a dirty blonde.

The first sentence means that her hair color was not dirty-blonde. The second sentence means she was not a blonde-haired girl in need of a bath.

The hyphen also changes the meaning of these sentences:

Papa Bear was a hot-porridge lover.
Papa Bear was a hot porridge lover.

The first sentence means that Papa Bear loved porridge at a high temperature. The second sentence means he was one sexy bear who loved porridge.

The hyphen can also help clarify meaning when used with the prefix *re*:

It's a good thing Goldilocks didn't try on the bears' clothes. Mama Bear would have been pissed if she had to *re-press* everything, and since she is a bear, she has a hard time *repressing* her anger.

The three bears sued Goldilocks for damages but couldn't *recover* all their losses because Goldilocks hired Gloria Allred to represent her. All the judge required Goldilocks to do was *re-cover* Baby Bear's chair because she got a porridge stain on it.

The closest we can get to set hyphen rules are that the prefixes *ex*, *self*, and *all* always require hyphens while adverbs ending in *ly* never do :

> **Goldilocks first told the jury that she had been walking through the *dimly lit* forest and mistook the three bears' house for an *all-inclusive* resort. When the jury seemed skeptical, she changed her story and said she had been in a *highly emotional* state and was suffering from low *self-esteem* because her *ex-boyfriend* Jack left her to climb a beanstalk.**

Exercise 8: Somebody's Been . . .

Directions: Add dashes and hyphens to the following things I would say if Goldilocks had broken into my house.

1. Somebody's been drinking and I mean really drinking my vodka.
2. Somebody's been watching my dirty movie collection.
3. Somebody's been sleeping in my water bed.
4. Somebody's been eating my Ben and Jerry's ice cream all three tubs.
5. Somebody's been reading my self help books.

The Scarlet Punctuation Mark: The Ellipsis

In high school, I was such a slut. And I was not alone; most girls in my high school were total sluts. We didn't sleep around or have loose morals, but for some reason, in high school, *slut* was the insult of choice. You were "a total slut" if you went to Homecoming with somebody's ex-boyfriend. You were even "a slut" if you hung out with someone who went to Homecoming with someone's ex-boyfriend. You were "a slut" if you were a cheerleader. You were "a slut" if you weren't a cheerleader. The only girls who managed to escape the slut label were the ones in band. Actually, that's not true: after *American Pie* came out, we learned what really happens at Band Camp.

The sad thing is that most of us haven't grown out of that immature high school behavior. In fact, we act just like the Puritan villagers from that book we had to read in high school, *The Scarlet Letter*. Just like the villagers made Hester Prynne wear a scarlet A to identify herself as an adulterer (which I think was totally unfair because she thought her husband was dead before she slept with the other guy), we treat the ellipsis like the town whore. The ellipsis mark is three little dots in a row (. . .), and we treat it like it will punctuate anything, anywhere, anytime. Have a look:

My schedule is up in the air at the moment . . . I am in town for sure until early September . . . but my grandma's 80th is in early October so I will probably be back in New York for that week . . . then after that I am not sure . . . I'm trying to figure that out . . . my lease will be up so I'm trying to figure out where to live . . . but I would love to see you if our schedules permit.

My friend who wrote this email spread those three little dots everywhere!

So how did the ellipsis get such a sordid reputation? Well, I guess the ellipsis *is* kind of a tease. When we see the ellipsis, we know that the sentence will not be consummated, but we know what's supposed to come next:

Sam is a respectable young man, but his friend Matt is, well . . .

I don't know exactly what the writer was going to say about Matt, but I can tell he's my kind of guy!

Or how about:

I wasn't going to go to the party tonight, but now that I know Matt is going to be there . . .

We don't need to finish that sentence with words to know where I'll be this evening.

And it probably doesn't help the ellipsis's reputation that we can also use it when we have a *pregnant* pause:

Let's just say Matt is . . . friendly.

We trail off or pause deeply in our writing only for dramatic effect; therefore, to avoid being drama kings and queens, we should rarely use the ellipsis for these purposes.

There is, however, one more use for the ellipsis: to indicate when words have been omitted from a word-for-word quotation. Sometimes in our writing, we include another person's words to help support our point, but we don't always need all of the words or sentences in a particular passage. However, we can't simply remove the words that don't serve our purpose; we have to at least let the reader know that they were there.

For example, let's say I am writing an essay for high school girls in which I am beseeching them to stop calling each other sluts. As I am writing this essay, I recall that there is a part in the movie *Mean Girls* in which the high school teacher played by Tina Fey expresses this same opinion. I decide that it would be a brilliant idea to include it in my essay to show my readers that this same sentiment has been expressed in a much-beloved movie. Here is the *Mean Girls* quote:

Ok, so we're all here 'cause of this book, right? Well, I don't know who wrote this book, but you all have got to stop calling each other sluts and whores. It just makes it ok for guys to call you sluts and whores. Who here has ever been called a slut?

The thing is I don't want to use the entire quote. I only want the second half of the second sentence and the last sentence. So here's how I would integrate it into my own writing:

The fact that *Mean Girls* addresses the issue of slut-calling in high school proves that it is still widespread. This issue is addressed when the math teacher gathers everyone together in an assembly and

says, "You all have got to stop calling each other sluts and whores. . . . Who here has ever been called a slut?" The fact that almost all students raised their hands shows that it affects most teenage girls.

The reason I didn't want to use the sentence **It just makes it ok for guys to call you sluts and whores** is that the point of that particular paragraph was that slut-calling is a widespread problem. At this point, I wasn't concerned with showing *why* it was a problem.

You may have noticed that instead of three dots after *whores*, there are four. That's because we omitted an entire sentence from the passage. The first dot isn't actually part of the ellipsis; it's the period that belongs to the sentence before the ellipsis.

The rule is that if you break at the end of a sentence, omit a sentence, and move to another, you must include the final punctuation mark from the first sentence, which, in some cases, could be a question mark (? . . .) or an exclamation point (! . . .).

- When omitting words from the middle of a sentence, we only use three dots:

Original: **Well, I don't know who wrote this book, but you all have got to stop calling each other sluts and whores.**

Ellipsis: **"you all have got to stop calling each other . . . whores."**

- We also use three dots when we omit words at the end of a sentence:

Original: **Well, I don't know who wrote this book, but you all have got to stop calling each other sluts and whores.**

Ellipsis: **"you all have got to stop calling each other sluts . . . "**

- We don't have to use the ellipsis when we omit words in the beginning of a sentence:

Original: **Well, I don't know who wrote this book, but you all have got to stop calling each other sluts and whores.**
Ellipsis: **"stop calling each other sluts and whores."**

So the moral of the story of the scarlet punctuation mark is that the ellipsis is not nearly as promiscuous as we think she is. She's definitely no comma—that curvy little seductress punctuates a hell of a lot more than the comparatively prude ellipsis.

Exercise 9: Give Her a Rest

Directions: To make up for our past treatment of the ellipsis, the least we can do is to give her a rest and replace her with the correct punctuation marks. Using the punctuation marks we have covered thus far (. , ; :), fix my friend's email.

> **My schedule is up in the air at the moment . . . I am in town for sure until early September . . . but my grandma's 80th is in early October so I will probably be back in New York for that week . . . then after that I am not sure . . . I'm trying to figure that out . . . my lease will be up so I'm trying to figure out where to live . . . but I would love to see you if our schedules permit.**

10

Mary Ann or Ginger: Punctuation with Quotation Marks

The girl next door or the voluptuous vamp? Perky or sexy? Short shorts or plunging neckline? Exclamation point or question mark?

Through my punctuation-colored glasses, that's how I see the *Gilligan's Island* ladies. Mary Ann reminds me of the perky, straightforward exclamation point and Ginger of the curvy, mysterious question mark.

How do you like your ladies and punctuation marks? Enthusiastic or elusive? Frisky or seductive?

I appreciate the exclamation point because it adds excitement to any sentence:

The Professor just made a radio out of a coconut!

Yet I appreciate the question mark because it provides mystique:

Is there something going on between the Professor and Mary Ann?

There is, however, one situation in which the line between the exclamation and the question is blurred: the rhetorical question. The asker of the rhetorical question isn't really expecting an answer; he or she is just using it for a dramatic effect. So, although it isn't grammatically incorrect to punctuate a rhetorical question with a question mark, the exclamation point is also acceptable:

Gilligan, do you think you could stop screwing up all of our attempts to get off the island!

In addition to both being acceptable punctuation for rhetorical questions, both the question mark and exclamation point act the same way around quotation marks. When only the quotation itself is a question or exclamation, the question mark and exclamation point are a bit more demure and hide inside the quotation marks. However, when the entire sentence is a question or exclamation, the question mark and exclamation point are more forward and expose themselves outside the quotation marks.

Confused? Come with me on this short voyage, and I'll show you what I mean:

In the following sentence, only the quotation is a question, so the question mark goes inside the quotation marks:

Mary Ann asked Ginger, "Why did you bring so many evening gowns on a three-hour tour?"

Similarly, in this next example, only the quotation is an exclamation, so like the question mark in the previous example, the exclamation point goes on the inside of the quotation marks:

Ginger replied, "At least I don't prance around day after day in daisy dukes!"

In this next sentence,the quotation isn't a question; the entire sentence is. Therefore, the question mark goes on the outside of the quotation marks:

Don't you love it when the Professor said brainy things like "It was a geological phenomenon caused by volcanic activity beneath the Earth's surface resulting into concentration of heat at a specific location"? And look—it's the same with the exclamation point when the whole sentence is an exclamation: **I do like the part about "concentration of heat at a specific location"!**

If Mary Ann is an exclamation point and Ginger is a question mark, then Gilligan would have to be the comma, right? Gilligan got roped into doing most of the manual labor on the island, and with all of its uses, the comma does much of the heavy lifting in sentences. The Professor would be the period. The period is a no-nonsense punctuation mark, and the Professor was the most rational of the castaways. (Although, how is it that the man could make explosives out of sand but could never fix a hole in a raft?)

Unlike the question mark and exclamation point, the comma and the period *always* sit inside the quotation marks:

The Skipper called Gilligan his "little buddy," but he made him do all the dirty work.
The Professor said things like "my eyes are ametropic and completely refractable."

Had the Minnow shipwrecked on the British Isle instead of Gilligan's Isle, however, the castaways would have been expected to place the period and comma outside the quotation marks because that's how they do it in Great Britain.

Exercise 10: Trouble in Paradise

Directions: If I were a special guest on *Gilligan's Island*, my character would try to turn all the castaways against each other. Punctuate my mischievous quotations correctly.

Here's what I would say . . .

1. To the Skipper: Gilligan may be your "little buddy" but I just heard him call you a "big jerk"
2. To Ginger: Can you believe that Mary Ann said in front of everyone, "Ginger's coconuts are fake"
3. To the Professor: Gilligan sure had nerve when he told Mary Ann, "The Professor learned all his tricks from me"
4. To Mary Ann: I just heard Ginger ask Mrs. Howell, "Don't you think wearing such tight shorts in such a hot climate would result in Mary Ann getting some kind of, you know, infection"
5. To Gilligan: The Skipper just hollered to the Professor, "Wait for me, little buddy"

That's Hot: Capitalization

A lot of us are fed up with large corporations these days. Their existence makes it nearly impossible for small businesses to thrive, they outsource jobs to other countries, they become too big to fail and then require a bailout. But what *really* irks me about large corporations is that they are responsible for the capitalization crisis that is currently plaguing our nation. Apple Inc. is the main culprit. Their iPods, iPhones, and iPads are so dang cool that to be just like them much of the nation has stopped capitalizing the word *I*. But Apple Inc. isn't the only offender. AT&T recently downsized their logo to at&t, and jetBlue not only neglects to capitalize the first letter of their name; they plop an inexplicable capital 'B' right in the middle of it.

The result: ChAoS. We no longer know which words require capitalization. Have a look:

- Copying the iPod, iMac, and iPhone model

Out of all the student emails I received last quarter, 80 percent of those students failed to capitalize their "I's." Here are just a couple of examples:

So, i was wondering if i could turn the extra credit in today.
I'm sorry i didn't make it today.
I am interested in what i got on my midterm.
i was wondering if i am supposed to come in to make up the final.

And if you think that's bad, check this out. It's real. I swear.

THANK YOU i WiLL WORK ON USiNG MORE SPECiFiC DETAiL iN MY PARAGRAPH SO THAT i WiLL GET A GOOD SCORE ON THAT SECTiON OF THE MiDTERM.

It's iMadness.

- Copying the at&t model

It's pretty much common knowledge that it's bad manners to write in all capital letters: IT'S LIKE YOU'RE YELLING AT YOUR READER! It's rude to yell, but that doesn't mean that you want to whisper. When you use all lower case letters, it makes your writing look, well, you know, um, kind of insecure, like this email I received from a student:

hi mrs. baranick,
i was wondering if you will accept my essay that was due yesterday. i'm really sorry i didn't get to make it to class. i fully understand if you won't accept it.

Because this student writes in all lower case, it looks like she doesn't even think she deserves the favor. And, if she doesn't think she deserves it, then why should I?

- Copying the jetBlue model

jetBlue may offer reasonable prices, plush leather seats, more legroom, and thirty-six channels of free DIRECTV, but does that give them the right to just have their way with capitalization? Just because I keep my seat belt fastened, keep my tray table up during take-off, and wait until the fasten seat belt sign turns off before I get up to retrieve my luggage, does that mean I'm entitled to have a smoke in the bathroom or help another with their oxygen mask *before* I put mine on? If jetBlue requires English teachers to follow their rules, then don't break ours! Here are the consequences of their rebellious behavior on today's impressionable youth:

> **Hello miss baranick,**
> **this is B_ _ _ _ K_ _ _ _ _ . I am in your monday class. I missed the Class today because I had to go to a funeral. I will come in Tuesday to get the assignment.**

She didn't capitalize my name, but she capitalized hers. Monday was not capitalized but Tuesday was. And why did she capitalize the word "class"? It's like she only returned one fourth of her seat to its upright position and left half of the tray table down.

Since big businesses have failed us, we need to look elsewhere for capitalization guidance. And who better than a woman who has made capitalization her specialty? With impressive tenacity, Paris Hilton has capitalized on her status as an heiress to achieve fame, fame, and fame. And the effort has paid off: today she has starred in her very own sex tape, reality show, music video, Carl's Jr. commercial, and is the author of the 2004 classic *Confessions of an Heiress*. In *Confessions of an Heiress*, she provides her readers with rules that must be followed to set free the heiress within. But you know what I think? I think she used the whole heiress thing as a cover, and what this book is really about is how to correctly apply the capitalization rules to our writing. Let's have a look at these rules:

Rule #1 – Have a great name.

If we were not given a particularly great name at birth, I guess we can change it to something more glamorous like Norma Jean Baker did when she changed her name to Marilyn Monroe. Or we may even want to change it to something fun like Caryn Johnson did when she became Whoopie Goldberg. Or why not just totally go for it like Dana Elaine Owens did when she changed her name to Queen Latifah? Or we can change it to something supercool like O'Shea Jackson did when he became Ice Cube. (See what I did there? Supercool. Ice Cube. Never mind.)

But now that I think about it, maybe that's not Paris's point. Maybe her point is that in order to access our inner heiress we have to believe that our name is great no matter what it is. And since all of our names are great, they deserve to be capitalized. We capitalize the names of people, places, and some things:

People: Paris Hilton
Places: Hilton Hotel
Things: Mercedes-Benz

This sounds simple enough, but sometimes when we're writing we may find ourselves asking the very same question Shakespeare's Juliet grappled with: "What is a name? (Okay, that's not true; her question was actually, "What's in a name?" but it was so close I thought you might not notice, and I would get some brownie points for referencing Shakespeare.) So where was I? Oh yes, we might find ourselves asking a question that Shakespeare's Juliet did not, in fact, grapple with, which is "What is a name?"

A name is a specific designation. For example, there are many nonspecific ways we could label someone: an heiress, a daughter of a billionaire, or a blonde. As you can see, these general descriptors are not capitalized because they don't refer to a unique entity. However, if you asked me *specifically* which one I was referring to, I would capitalize her name: Ivanka Trump. Oops! I mean, Paris Hilton.

And to be honest with you, sometimes I am not sure if a word is general or specific. For example, the other day I wanted to write the word *geisha* (I was not applying for the job. I swear.), and I wasn't sure whether or not it should be capitalized. So I just did a Google search to see if other websites (reliable websites, not random blogs about geisha fetishes) capitalized it. It turns out *geisha* is not capitalized—nor does it pay very well.

Rule #2 – Be born into the right family.

Do I love my family? Yes. Was I born into the right family? I'm not convinced. I wonder what bad karma I accumulated in my past life to make it so I wasn't reincarnated into a family of billionaire hoteliers.

So does that mean that we only capitalize words of family relationships if we were born into the right family?

No, it's not that simple; families never are.

Most of the time, in fact, we don't capitalize the words of family relationships. We only do if we are using the word as a substitute for the person's name:

Hey, Sis, don't you think Mom and Dad should have started a hotel chain?

We capitalize Sis, Mom, and Dad because we could also have used their names:

Hey, Cindy, don't you think Carol and Greg should have started a hotel chain?

We don't, however, capitalize words of family relationships when we are not directly addressing the family member or are not able to substitute their names. A safe rule to go by is not to capitalize the word of family relationship if it has a *my, our, your, their, her,* or *his* in front of it:

***My* sister and I are pissed that *our* mom and dad didn't start a hotel chain.**

Let's run it through the plug-in-their-names test:

My Cindy and I are pissed that our Carol and Greg didn't start a hotel chain.

It didn't pass the test, so no capitalization.

Rule #3 – Eat only fast food or the most fabulous food.

At first, I was like, "WHAT!" I understood the fabulous food, but heiresses eating fast food? But then I realized that it makes perfect sense. I don't care how divine caviar and foie gras supposedly taste; there is nothing more delicious than a greasy cheeseburger and fries. And since heiresses can afford to hire the best personal trainers, or better yet, a quick liposuction, why not indulge?

Plus, when you think about it, heiresses are busy people. They don't get out of bed until 11 AM, and that doesn't leave a ton of time for manicures, clothes shopping, shoe shopping, massages, and Botox. So when they can't fit in the fabulous food before the massage, they simply must take the limo through the drive-through.

With such busy schedules, it makes sense that heiresses would love all fast things; therefore, it makes sense that they would also love fast words. I'm talking about abbreviations. Therefore, whenever we use an abbreviation, we capitalize it:

Word Spelled Out	Abbreviation
Television	TV
compact disc	CD
public display of affection	PDA

Rule #4 – Develop a way of entering the room that looks regal but not snobby.

For an heiress that means shoulders back, chin up, tiara straight. For our writing, there's nothing more regal than entering a sentence by capitalizing the first letter of the first word. Capitalizing the entire word would be snobby. I mean, look at this:

GOOD morning, Jeeves; bring me my morning mimosa.

Obnoxious!
Not capitalizing it makes it look rather common:

good morning, Jeeves; bring me my morning mimosa.

But capitalizing the first letter of the first word:

Good morning, Jeeves; bring me my morning mimosa.

Now, that's regal.

Rule #5 – Never ever wake up before ten, and never go to bed before three.

I really hope she's talking about 3 PM. Some of us heiresses have to work in the morning. We can't all just party like it's 1999.

Speaking of partying like it's 1999, does that still mean to party like crazy, or does that mean to party whilst wearing a belly shirt and dancing to Britney Spears's "Hit Me Baby One More Time?"

And speaking of 1999, can you believe it's already been over ten years since then, which means we are in the twenty-first century? And speaking of centuries, do we capitalize them? Well, we do capitalize periods of time when we are referring to a specific era:

Victorian Era
Renaissance Era
Paleozoic Era
But, we don't capitalize the century numbers:
nineteenth century

Rule #6 – Always tell everyone what they want to hear.

That nondesigner dress is absolutely divine.

World peace is very important to me.

I had no idea that sex tape would be released.

Heiresses, you *are* good, but the one group of people that beats you hands down when it comes to telling people what they want to hear is politicians. Therefore, we capitalize many words pertaining to politics. We, for example, capitalize the names of governmental offices:

Congress

House of Representatives

Senate

Supreme Court

We capitalize the names of political parties:

Democratic Party

Republican Party

Green Party (No, that's not the money party.)

We don't, however, capitalize political philosophies because they are referring to general concepts rather than the name of a specific entity:

democracy

republic

liberty

capitalism

socialism

materialism

Rule #7 – Make plans, plans, and more plans.

Shopping, massages, pedicures, oh my! The Hamptons, Maui, Vegas, why not?

Heiresses can do whatever their hearts desire *Monday* to *Sunday*, *January* to *December*.

Therefore, we capitalize the days of the week and the months of the year.

Rule #8 – Act Ditzy; Lose Things.

(Giggle, giggle). Ooops! I didn't know that a margarita had alcohol in it. You mean the video recorder aimed at us was actually on? Where did I leave my tiara?

You see, people might start to expect things of an heiress, someone with the power and prestige to make a difference and serve as a role model for today's youth. Such expectations might interfere with sleeping in, shopping, and clubbing. That's not hot!

The best thing you can do is to pretend you don't know up from down, left from right, here from there. So why bother capitalizing directions? They don't matter.

We do not, therefore, capitalize: **north, south, east, or west** if they are simply referring to compass directions.

For example:

Go west on Sunset Boulevard, and then go north on the freeway.
Did you get all that, Jeeves?

The only time we capitalize the words north, south, east, or west is if they are referring to an actual geographic location. For example, we capitalize places like Northern California, Southern California, the South, the Northeast, West Germany, and East Germany because we are referring to a specific region, not a compass direction.

Let's spend this summer on a yacht in the South of France.

Yes, let's!

Rule #9 – Always have a very big bodyguard.

Now, don't get me wrong; I love the idea of having my own personal bouncer. It would be splendid to have someone to scare off the Greenpeace guys waiting to ambush me in front of Whole Foods so I could enjoy my $20 juice in peace. I'm just worried that having a big, scary-looking guy attached to my hip might distract my students from my grammar lectures. I would also probably have to get him some special pass to be on campus. Plus, how much does a bodyguard cost these days?

So for those of you who, like me, don't see an actual bodyguard as a viable option, I have come up with some alternatives:

First of all, for those of us who are religious, we can claim our god as our bodyguard. Like a bodyguard, a god watches over us, right? So the big question is whether or not we capitalize the word *god*.

We do not capitalize *god* when we are talking about the concept of god in general. For example,

I may select Thor as the *god* to protect me. He looks pretty bad ass.

We do, however, capitalize it when we are actually addressing God or using God as a name. For example,

I believe that *God* will protect me from all of the paparazzi.

We also capitalize names of various gods:

Buddha, Yahweh, Zeus

We also capitalize religions:

Christianity, Judaism, Hindu, Islam, Paganism

For those of us who don't consider ourselves religious, then what about the president? He's supposed to keep us safe, right? So do we capitalize the word *president?* We capitalize it when we are using the word as a title with his (and hopefully one day her) name. For example:

Who do you think could bench press more, *President* Washington or *President* Jefferson?

But, we don't capitalize it otherwise:

The *president* of the United States should have to be able to bench press at least 200 lbs.

For those of us who aren't really religious and don't trust the government, we will have to look inside of ourselves and access our inner strength. Therefore, we always capitalize the word *I.*

Rule #10 – Never be predictable.

In her book, Paris gives a list of her favorite books: *Sex and the City*, by Candace Bushnell; *Ultimate Style: the Best of the Best-Dressed List*, by Betina Zhika, and absolutely anything by Jackie Collins. I must admit that it was a little unpredictable that Paris reads books, but the fact that her faves are all books about fashion and full of drama isn't all that shocking. But there is one surprising book on that list: it's a novel, a classic, it contains themes and symbolism and big words like *meretricious*, *punctilious*, and *redolent.* Paris Hilton loves *The Great Gatsby*, by F. Scott Fitzgerald! Oh Paris, you *are* such an unpredictable heiress!

You will notice that when you look at the titles of Paris's favorite books some of the words are capitalized and some are not. Most people think that you just don't capitalize small words in titles; I wish it were that simple. You do capitalize some small words in titles (and this goes for the titles of anything: movies, TV shows, songs, essays, etc.). Here are the rules:

Rule 1 – Always capitalize the **first** and **last** word in a title.

Rule 2 – Don't capitalize **a, an,** or **the** (unless they are the first or last word).

- *Sex and the City*
- *The Great Gatsby*

Rule 3 – Don't capitalize the FANBOYS. Remember those FANBOYS? They are none other than the **for, and, nor, but, or, yet, so** we met in the comma chapter. (Only capitalize them if they are the first or last word in the title.)

- Sex **and** the City
- **And** Then Came Morning

Rule 4 – Don't capitalize short prepositions (unless they are the first or last word). If you don't recall the definition of a preposition, that's no problem; I've got it right here for you: Prepositions are little words that usually express where or when. These are the most common prepositions found in titles and should get you by:

to, in, on, with, by, of, from, at

And all can be aptly used in a title for Paris's infamous sex tape:

*Been **to** Paris*

*Been **in** Paris*

*Been **on** Paris*

*Been **with** Paris*

*Been **by** Paris*

*All **of** Paris*

*Paris: Live **at** the Bellagio*

*Just came **from** Paris*

So that means if a word in a title is small but not an article, a short preposition, or a FANBOYS, such as **am, is, you, me,** we capitalize it.

Rule #11 – Never have roots in your hair.

I agree about the hair, but I'd like to remind heiresses that all roots are not bad. In fact, it's important that heiresses appreciate their roots, for if it weren't for their roots, heiresses wouldn't be heiresses.

Also, Paris Hilton should thank her great-grandfather for her Scandinavian roots because it makes it seem more plausible that she is a natural blonde.

So, in honor of our roots, we capitalize our ethnicity. For example:

Spanish

Asian

European

Hispanic

African American

Caucasian

Instead of *African American* and *Caucasian*, some of us use *black* and *white*. While most writing style guides don't capitalize *black* and *white*, there is an ongoing discussion about it. So, here's what I advise: follow your own sense of style. If you want to capitalize *Black* and *White*, go for it. If you don't want to capitalize *black* and *white*, don't. Just be consistent!

Rule #12 – Never go out the night after the Oscars.

The Oscars air on Sunday night, and Monday night is a school night for me. That is why I never go out the night after the Oscars. However, that's probably not why Paris probably doesn't. I imagine that for celebrities going out the night after the Oscars would be like dressing slutty the night after Halloween—totally anti-climactic. I mean, how can a short skirt and a low-cut top compete with a slutty nurse's costume?

The Oscars are like Hollywood's Halloween. Everyone gets all dressed up, cakes on makeup, and goes to parties. It's a holiday! Since we love holidays, we capitalize them:

Christmas

Valentine's Day

Kwanzaa

Mardi Gras

Rule #13 – Never go out when it's raining unless you have a Gucci umbrella.

And, whatever you do, don't forget your Burberry raincoat, your Hermés scarf, your Prada boots, your Louis Vuitton handbag, and your Chanel gloves! Brand names are everything, so of course we capitalize them.

Also, sometimes neglecting to capitalize brand names can be misleading. For example:

I love coke; it gives me a boost of energy.

I'm sure she meant Coke, as in Coca-Cola, as in the soda pop . . . right?

Rule #14 – Never spend the summer in New York or the winter in the Hamptons.

Yeah, I know, totally, right? I would never spend summer in New York. How lame! And only amateurs would touch foot in the Hamptons December through March because it's just so . . .

Actually, I have no idea why winter in the Hamptons is a faux pas. Another thing I don't understand is why we don't capitalize summer or winter, or any of the other seasons for that matter. It seems like we should, but spring, summer, fall, and winter are all lowercase.

Rule #15 – Go out with broke guys. Money doesn't matter if they're nice.

Whew! I am so relieved that Paris is so down-to-earth. I am glad she understands that money isn't everything. It must be a coincidence that two of her boyfriends were heirs to shipping tycoons. They must have both been really, really nice.

So, since it doesn't matter if he's a doctor, lawyer, movie producer, or hamburger flipper, we don't typically capitalize names of careers. In fact, the only time we do capitalize the name of a career is if it is used as part of a person's name (as a title).

For example,

- **Which doctor do you go to for your Botox treatment?**
  I go to Doctor Morgan.
- **Professor Green is on the phone!**
  What's a professor?

All this talk about careers has got me thinking: how do heiresses feel about education? Well, it looks like they have different opinions. Some heiresses, like our own Ms. Hilton, dropped out of high school, but some, like Ms. Trump, have received a formal education. Not surprisingly, this ambivalence toward education reflects in the capitalization rules: some education-related words we capitalize, while others we don't. Here are the rules:

- Only capitalize the words high school, college, and university when they are used as part of the name.

I'm going to send my kids to West Beverly High School.
You can't. That's a make-believe high school from *Beverly Hills 90210.*

- Do not capitalize the words **freshman**, **sophomore**, **junior**, or **senior**.

Even if I met Dylan when he was a *senior* and I was a *freshman*, he would still totally dump Brenda for me.

- Don't capitalize the names of subjects or majors, but do capitalize the names of classes.

I want to be a fashion designer.
Why don't you study fashion design? You should take Fashion Design 101.

I think I'll just buy my own fashion line.

Note: The only time you capitalize the name of a subject or a major is if it is a language.

If I did go to college, obviously I would major in French.

- Capitalize academic degrees only when the **abbreviation** or the **specific name** of the degree is used, such as **Bachelor of Arts (BA)** or **Master of Science (MS)**, or **Doctor of Philosophy (PhD)**. General references, such as bachelor's, master's, or doctoral degree, are not capitalized.

For example,

Remember the apostrophe

↓

- **I have a bachelor's degree.**

Does that mean that you're, like, really good at not being married?

I have a BA ← Abbreviation

You have a bare ass?

No, I have a Bachelor of Arts. ← Specific name

Thank you, Paris, for teaching us the rules of capitalization. Thanks to you, we will capitalize our way to success in our essays, cover letters, résumés, proposals, and emails. Or I guess we could just make a sex tape.

Exercise 11: If I Were a Rich Girl . . .

Directions: For those of you who are pretty sure a sex tape is not in your future, here's an exercise to test your capitalization skills. Underline the capitalization errors.

1. I would go to the westin hotel in new york city and order their $1000 bagel. It is topped with White Truffle Cream Cheese and infused with goji berries and golden leaves.
2. I would find the person who bought the pair of stuart weitzman shoes from harrods in london for $1.5 million and offer them $2 million. How could I not? The shoes are woven from Platinum and set with 626 rubies. Plus, they were inspired by my favorite movie, *The Wizard Of Oz*.
3. To go with my new sparkly shoes, I would blow $5 million on the new bra from victoria's secret called the black diamond fantasy miracle bra.
4. To deal with the harsh Autumn and Winter months we experience in southern california, I would buy a $50,000 Crocodile Skin umbrella.
5. Since i love vacationing in the bahamas, hawaii, and jamaica, I would buy my own Island. And i'm in luck. The island vatu varu, located in Fiji, is on sale for the reasonable price of $40 million.

12

Freudian Slip: Using You

I don't agree with Freud's theory about women having penis envy. Don't get me wrong, gentlemen; your penises are great. I'm just personally not interested in possessing one myself. To be honest, the last thing I need is to worry about the size of another one of my body parts. But just because I don't envy penises doesn't mean that I disagree with all of Freud's theories. For example, I totally agree with Freud's theory about projection.

Freud believed that projection is a psychological defense mechanism whereby we "project" our own desires and thoughts onto someone else. For example, if your partner is thinking about cheating, he or she will "project" this desire onto you and suspect you of cheating. And this brings me to another reason I don't believe in penis envy: no one would envy my husband's penis if I found out he was cheating.

I agree with Freud's theory about projection, though, because my students do it all the time. In their essays, they claim that they are talking about me, but I know that they are actually just talking about themselves. For example, one of my students wrote an essay about her trip to Italy, and here's one of her sentences:

When *you* first see Michelangelo's *David*, the first thing *you* notice is the craftsmanship.

Well, I have news for this student. I have also been to Italy and have seen Michelangelo's *David.* In fact, here's a picture I took of it:

Let's just say that the craftsmanship wasn't the very first thing *my* eyes were drawn to.

Instead of using *you,* she has a couple of options. If she was assigned to write an autobiographical piece, she should have used *I* because she was talking about her own point of view, not mine:

When *I* first saw Michelangelo's David, the first thing *I* noticed was the craftsmanship.

If she was assigned a traditional academic essay, she should stay away from using both *I* and *you.* Instead, she should use the *she*, *he*, *it*, *they,* and *them.*

These words we use all the time like *I, you, me, she, he, him, her, it, they,* and *them* are called pronouns. We use these words to take the place as noun substitutes because if we didn't, trust me, it would get annoying. Here's an example of a group of pronoun-free sentences:

When Linda and Brad went to Italy, Linda and Brad went to see Michelangelo's *David.* The first thing Brad noticed about the

David **was the** ***David's*** **craftsmanship. Let's just say that Linda's eyes were drawn to the** ***David's*** **manship, not the** ***David's*** **craftsmanship, but Linda was too embarrassed to tell Brad because Linda didn't want Brad to think that Linda had a one-track mind. As a result, Linda averted Linda's eyes and commented on the masterful use of the marble.**

Here's how it looks with pronouns:

When Linda and Brad went to Italy, they went to see Michelangelo's ***David.*** **The first thing Brad noticed about the** ***David*** **was its craftsmanship. Let's just say that Linda's eyes were drawn to the** ***David's*** **manship, not its craftsmanship, but Linda was too embarrassed to tell Brad because she didn't want him to think that she had a one-track mind. As a result, she averted her eyes and commented on the masterful use of the marble.**

Much better!

Pronouns are categorized by person: first, second, and third:

First	I, me, my, we, us
Second	you, your
Third	he, she, it, his, her, its, they, them, their

Academic and formal writing typically call for the third person. Here's how to express my student's sentence in the third person.

When someone sees Michelangelo's ***David*** **for the first time,** ***he*** **or** ***she*** **may immediately note the exquisite craftsmanship.**

Notice that I included the word *may* in the sentence above? We can't say for certain what someone else would notice.

Also, notice that in the second half of the sentence it says ***he*** **or** ***she*** *may immediately note the exquisite craftsmanship*. The tendency would be to use *they* instead of *he* or *she*, which would look like this:

Incorrect: **When someone sees Michelangelo's *David* for the first time, *they* may immediately note the exquisite craftsmanship.**

However, this is technically incorrect because the pronoun is substituting *someone*, which is singular. *They*, on the other hand, is plural.

There was a time when we would have simply deferred to the masculine pronoun *he*, which would have looked like this:

Incorrect: **When someone sees Michelangelo's *David* for the first time, *he* may immediately note the exquisite craftsmanship.**

But then somebody realized that half of the population wasn't male, so deferring to the masculine pronoun is now considered sexist. So until we come up with a singular pronoun that refers to both males and females (shhe?) we are stuck with the clunky expression *he or she*.

In the case of this sentence, there is one more option. We can change the subject from singular to plural, and consequently, make the pronoun plural:

When *people* see Michelangelo's *David* for the first time, *they* may immediately note the exquisite craftsmanship.

But my main point is that we must be careful when using *you* in our writing because we don't want to turn off our readers by making it look like we're assuming too much about them. For example, another student wrote an essay on STD prevention, and this was one of his sentences:

When you experience a herpes flare-up, it's important to refrain from sexual activity.

Well, um, this is awkward. My student is insinuating that I have herpes. That's a bit inappropriate, don't you think? Let me just put a little minus sign after that letter grade.

This student definitely should have avoided using *you*. And even if he had herpes, he probably shouldn't have used *I* either—there are simply some things a teacher needn't know about her students. And I don't actually think my student was trying to say that he had herpes. I think he was just unaware. Instead of indicating whom he was really referring to, he took a shortcut, like many of us do, and used *you*. He should have written something like this:

> **When *people suffering from herpes* experience a flare-up, *they* should refrain from sexual activity.**

This doesn't mean that we should never use *you* in our writing; it just means that we should use it wisely. It's entirely appropriate to use *you* when directly addressing our readers. For example, it's common to use *you* when writing a how-to manual, a guidebook, or a recipe because we are actually telling our readers what to do. For example:

> **First, you add one shot of tequila.**
> **Next, you add one more shot of tequila.**

Using *you* is also an effective technique to use in advertising because we want our target customer to feel connected to the product. For example, Burger King effectively uses you in its slogan *We Do It Your Way*. Why, thank you, Burger King. I appreciate that. Now, if we could just get the rest of the world to do it my way, we'd really be in business.

Basically, using *you* in our writing creates an intimacy with our readers. Therefore, before we use it, we really need to think about whether or not we want to connect with our readers on that level. If it's our college professor, we probably don't. If it's our business colleague, I doubt it. But I've thought about it, and now that we're seven chapters deep into this book, I'm ready to connect with you, dear readers, on that level. Here it goes:

How are you?

Are you enjoying the book?

What's your sign?

Exercise 12: Stop Projecting

Directions: Fill in the blanks using pronouns *he, she, they* whenever possible. There's only one condition: don't use the word *you.*

1. When ______ first meet me, the first thing ______ notice is ______.
2. ______ would be surprised by my ability to ______.
3. If someone had met me five years ago, ______ would have noticed my ______.
4. When people first learn that I'm ______, ______tend to react by ______.
5. It's better if ______ don't interrupt me when I'm______; if ______ do, I might ______.

13

How Old Do You Think I Am?: Numbers

When I was little, I was so accurate with numbers. When someone would ask my age, I would answer, "I'm five and three quarters and seven days and three hours." Ask me today, and I'd say twenty-nine—the same age I have been claiming for the past five years. I think it's fair to say that as we get older we start manipulating numbers to suit our needs.

- **Boyfriend:** How many guys have you been with?
- **Girlfriend:** Quite a few more than the number I am about to give you.
- **Girl:** How tall are you?
- **Boy:** I'm 5 foot 11 . . . I mean, 6 foot.
- **Driver's License Renewal Form Question:** Weight?
- **Me:** The number I am going to weigh after I finish the diet I will be starting tomorrow.

I partially blame this numbers-gone-wild attitude for our confusion regarding how to express numbers when we write. However, many of us are confused about when to actually spell out the number or when to use the symbol because there's really no accepted industry consensus. Some writing style guides require us to spell out the number if it can be expressed in two words or fewer (e.g., twenty-nine, seven, one hundred). Others require us to only spell out the numbers less than 10 (29, seven, 100). Others require us to use Roman numerals within XIV minutes of eating Italian food (XXIX, VII, C).

Instead of throwing our arms up in the air and cursing the English language gods for making everything so confusing, let's make this work in our favor. Here's what you do: Tell your boss that it's of the utmost importance that your company adopts a consistent policy regarding how to express numbers in writing. Explain that an uneducated and inconsistent approach to expressing numbers makes the company's writing look sloppy. Next, tell your boss that you'd consider taking on the role as CNO of the company. At this point, your boss will probably ask what a CNO is. To this, you reply, "The chief numbers officer. All the cool companies have created this new position to ensure the consistent expression of numbers in their company's documents." Then cross your fingers that your boss doesn't call up all the cool companies and ask. Of course, your new added responsibility of making sure all numbers are expressed correctly and consistently would require a substantial raise.

Your first responsibility as CNO is to decide which of the following rules you'd like to adopt:

1. Writing out all numbers that are expressed in two words or fewer and using numerals for all numbers that are expressed in three words or more.

or

2. Only writing out numbers one through nine and using numerals for any number greater than nine.

or

3. Write out all numbers from one to ninety-nine and use numerals for all the others.

Choosing your number style, however, is only the beginning. Once you've got that, you must contend with the fact that there are as many exceptions to that rule as there are to jetBlue's $29 flight deals. You know what I'm talking about, right? You get an email boasting $29 fares and you excitedly call up your friend in Portland and tell her you'll finally get to visit until you read further and discover that such fares only apply on Tuesday, at 3:33 AM, when Jupiter is rising in Saturn.

Your added challenge as CNO is that your office probably has some overachievers who might struggle with the exceptions. These overachievers—those annoying coworkers who laugh at all the boss's jokes and do those over-the-top PowerPoint presentations—will probably also want to impress the boss by writing out all of the numbers, no matter how many words they may be. Please impress upon them that no one, not even the boss, wants to read the number four million six hundred thirty-two thousand four hundred and thirty-two. And also let them know that numerals are actually preferred under the following circumstances:

- Dates, ages, and decades
  *I was born on **December 27, 197** . . . I mean **1982**. That makes me **29** years old. As I mentioned before, I was born in the **1980s**. Please notice that I did not write **1980's** with the apostrophe—that would have been incorrect because nothing belongs to the **1980s**.*

- Weight and dimensions
  *I am **5 foot 9 inches** tall, have a **39-inch** bust, an **18-inch** waist, **33-inch** hips, and weigh **110 pounds**.*
  Okay, fine, those are Barbie's dimensions, not mine. But if I keep doing my side bends and repeating my "must increase my bust mantra," maybe one day.

- Addresses

  *My future address will be **1600 Pennsylvania Avenue NW, Washington D.C. 20500**.*

  As your first female president, I will change America's dessert from apple pie to chocolate and America's national pastime from baseball to shopping. I also vow to put an end to gender stereotypes.

- Consistency

  Make sure numbers are consistent only if they are referring to the same thing in the same sentence. In these examples, the numbers are both referring to inches:

  *I didn't believe him when he said that it only grew **2 inches** in high school but **12 inches** in college.*

  Or

  *I didn't believe him when he said that it only grew **two inches** in high school but **twelve inches** in college.*

  Then, he showed me a picture, and his hair was, in fact, all the way down his back by the time he was a college senior.

Once you've dealt with the overachievers, you'll have to make sure the slackers—your coworkers who surf the web all day and tend to fall ill on Mondays—understand that a number must be written out under the following circumstance:

- When it starts a sentence

  ***Seventeen million four hundred thirty-three thousand two hundred and twenty-two orgasms** are faked every day.*

  However, to avoid writing out such a long number, try rearranging the sentence, like this:

  *Every day, **17,433,222** orgasms are faked.*

  Or try expressing your needs to your partner.

- Two numbers next to each other

  How was your fishing trip?

  Great! I caught ***12 36****-inch salmon.*

  You caught salmon that were ***1,236*** *inches long!*

  No, I caught ***twelve 36****-inch . . . I mean, yes.*

Congratulations! You now have the required knowledge to become CNO of any company. Isn't this exciting? Your company appears more professional, and you get job security and a few extra bucks with which you can buy me a fabulous gift for my big twenty-ninth birthday bash.

Exercise 13: Lie to Me

Directions: But before you approach your boss, let's make sure you've really got it. Fill in the blank with the number of your choice.

1. I have ____________________ Facebook friends.
2. ____________________ people asked me for my autograph on the way here.
3. I can bench press ____________________ pounds.
4. My favorite decade is the ____________________.
5. I kissed ____________________ people this year compared with ____________________ people last year.

14

Keepin' It Real: Grammar Myth Busting

Sometimes when I am standing in front of a classroom full of students, I get drunk.

Not drunk with alcohol, my friends—drunk with power. These students, I think to myself, will believe anything I tell them about grammar because I am their grammar teacher. I could tell them that it's grammatically incorrect to start a sentence with the word *Tuesday* between 10 AM and 3 PM on every second Tuesday because of street sweeping. I could tell them that three exclamation points are required after every sentence that includes the word *snowman* on Christmas Day.

How do I know they'd believe me? Because we've been believing grammar quacks for years. Since the eighteenth century, there have been various special interest groups spreading grammar myths to achieve their dubious purposes. And we've largely accepted these myths as truth.

However, it's time to bust these myths open and expose the following special interest groups as the lie-spreading machines that they are:

Latin Lovers: adhering too closely to the rules

I'm not talking about Don Juan DeMarco; he can punctuate however he wants as far as I'm concerned. I'm talking about people who love the Latin language.

One of these Latin lovers was an eighteenth-century English clergyman named Robert Lowth. His understanding of grammar was based largely on the study of Latin, which would have been fine except for the fact that he decided to *carpe diem* and write a largely influential English grammar book based on Latin rules. One such rule he propagated was that we must never end a sentence with a preposition.

A preposition is a word that typically indicates time or space. Some that we commonly use to end sentences are *at*, *for*, *with*, *from*, *in*, and *on*.

This is a sentence that ends in a preposition:

I left my door unlocked so Don Juan could sneak *in*.

Latin Lovers might suggest that we rewrite it like this:

I left my door unlocked so *in* Don Juan could sneak.

I don't know about you, but if someone said that to me, I'd kind of want to punch them in their pretentious little mouth.

Not only can rearranging our sentences to avoid ending them in prepositions sound pretentious, it's also unnecessary. Grammar experts agree that it's perfectly acceptable to end sentences in prepositions.

It is, however, grammatically incorrect to end a sentence with a preposition if the preposition is unnecessary.

In the example above, we needed the preposition because without it the sentence wouldn't make sense:

I left my door unlocked so Don Juan can sneak.

However, in the following sentence, the preposition is unnecessary:

When Don Juan left, he asked, "Do you know where I left my sword *at*?"

If we leave off the *at*, the sentence still makes sense:

When Don Juan left, he asked, "Do you know where I left my sword?"

So Don Juan's use of the preposition was wrong.

But English is his second language, so be easy on him. He's learning.

The Wedding Industry: overdoing formality

Marriages are declining drastically in the United States. I blame Kim Kardashian. If she can't maintain a marriage for over seventy-two hours, what hope in hell do the rest of us have? However, studies show a different reason: today, it's socially acceptable to live with someone without being married.

This is bad news for the wedding industry. If this trend continues, how are the wedding planners, cake makers, penis-shaped paraphernalia businesses, and divorce lawyers going to survive?

The wedding industry has a vested interest in making sure that we value formal relationships (marriages) over informal relationships (dating), which leads me to my theory: the wedding industry, in a desperate attempt to promote the value of formality over informality, has spread the grammar myth that it's incorrect to start a sentence with the words *and* or *but*.

I'm not just a crazy conspiracy theorist. Hear me out:

Sentences, much like couples, have ways to demonstrate their relationship statuses. Couples use engagement and wedding rings; sentences use transitional words and phrases.

Here are some common transitional words and phrases:

for example, therefore, however, consequently, moreover, furthermore

By beginning a sentence with a transitional word, the sentence is telling the world about its relationship with the sentence that it follows.

For example, if a sentence begins with the word *furthermore*, it's letting everyone know that it is giving additional information about what was said in the previous sentence:

I must have swans at my wedding. *Furthermore*, I would like doves.

If a sentence starts with the word *however*, its relationship will be "in spite of" what was stated in the previous sentence:

Doves will break our budget. *However*, I think they're worth it.

I love transitional words and phrases like the ones listed above. I use them all the time, and I highly recommend you use them too. But there are times when I find those particular words a tad too formal for the writing style I am trying to achieve, and that's when I like to start my sentences with the more informal transitional words *and* and *but.*

If we don't have a wedding and just move in together, we will save thousands of dollars. *And* we will save on rent.
My parents think that we should get married. *But* I think that marriage is just a contract.

The good news is that, despite what the wedding industry would have you believe, it's grammatically acceptable to create less formal relationships between sentences by beginning them with *and* and *but.*

Swans, however, are a must!

Teenagers: because what?

If the following exchanges sound familiar to you, you'll understand why teenagers started the rumor that it's wrong to start a sentence with the word *because:*

Teen: Dad, can I go to a concert tonight with my friends?

Dad: No, you have to finish your homework.

Teen: I'm done with my homework.

Dad: It's a school night.

Teen: It's Friday.

Dad: Concerts are dangerous.

Teen: This one is at my friend's church.

Dad: Will there be adults there?

Teen: It will be mostly adults.

Dad: You can't go.

Teen: Why not?

Dad: **Because** I said so.

Obviously, teens have spread this rumor in an attempt to prevent their parents from uttering the most frustrating combination of words in the entire world: *because I said so.*

Although sentences can start with the word *because*, the teens are right about one thing: *because I said so* is not a complete sentence. When we start sentences with the word *because*, there is the tendency to incorrectly form incomplete sentences. Here's an example:

I had to stay home on Friday night. Because my lame dad wouldn't let me go to the concert. My friends all think I am a total dork.

Because my lame dad wouldn't let me go to the concert is not a complete sentence. However, if we connect it to the sentence that follows it, it is:

Because my lame dad wouldn't let me go to the concert, my friends all think I am a total dork.

When a sentence starts with the word *because*, it will be the kind of sentence that we talked about in the comma chapter on page 51. It will have the following structure:

Introductory phrase, complete sentence.

So, teens, let's compromise. Instead of spreading the myth that we can NEVER start a sentence with the word because, let's say that *because* will never start a sentence when it doesn't begin an introductory phrase that is followed by a comma and a complete sentence.

It's a win/win. I get to promote grammatical correctness and *because I said so* is still grammatically incorrect.

Health Freaks: pushing wellness.

When these people are offered a cookie, they don't automatically stuff it in their mouth; they decline it based on its caloric and saturated fat content. When these people are offered a shot of tequila, they don't down it in one gulp and ask for another; they decline it based on the fact that alcohol is bad for the liver. When these people wake up on Sunday morning, they don't head to the nearest bacon and pancake outlet; they head to the gym. These health freaks must be the ones who started the false rumor that it's grammatically incorrect to answer the question "how are you?" with "good" instead of "well."

I don't think they did it maliciously. It's just that to these people health is the only thing that matters. So when someone asks them how they are, they simply assume that the person is inquiring about the state of their health. Consequently, they answer "I'm well."

When used to describe ourselves, *well* means *in good health.* And it's perfectly acceptable to answer a "how are you?" with an "I'm well." However, it's also perfectly acceptable to give an answer that reflects your overall state of being, and, therefore, "good" is also acceptable. If we answer, "I am good," it means we're not terrible, but we're not fantastic.

But we will be fantastic after that cookie, tequila, and bacon!

Congratulations! You are now part of the Right Club. You now know that you are perfectly in the right to express yourself in ways that others have tried to convince you are wrong. The first rule of Right Club, however, is that not everyone knows about the Right Club. This means that even though you know you are right other people may still believe these myths and think you are wrong. These other people may include your bosses, teachers, and clients. So until these grammatical truths become common knowledge, when your boss asks how you are, perhaps you want to answer as though he or she is inquiring after your health.

Exercise 14: Bust It Up

Directions: Now that the grammar myths have been busted, answer the following questions in ways you may have previously thought wouldn't digest for seven years.

1. Your friends asks, "How are you?"

Your answer: ______________________

2. Your client asks, "How are you?"

Your answer ______________________

3. "Why did the chicken cross the road?" (Circle the only INCORRECT answer.)
   A. Because it wanted to get to the other side.
   B. Because the chicken wanted to get to the other side, it crossed the road.
   C. Chickens love to explore both sides of roads.
4. Which is the only annoying question from your parents that is grammatically correct?
   A. What have you gotten yourself into?
   B. Where are you going to?
   C. Where is the party at?
5. Fill in the blanks with your choice of the following transitions:

however, and, but, furthermore, moreover, nonetheless

   A. My mom always told me not to swallow my gum because it would stay in my stomach for seven years. __________ she told me that if I sit too close to the TV I will eventually go blind.
   B. My friends told me that if I look in the mirror and say "Bloody Mary" three times in a row a ghost will appear in the mirror. I don't believe them. ____________ I will never try it—just in case.

15

Avoid Premature Ejaculation: Email Etiquette

It happened to me the other day. It was so embarrassing. I was sending an email to an editor concerning a job I wanted. The editor was named Stephen; I addressed it to Steven. I noticed this stupid error only *after* I had clicked *Send* and my email was to irretrievably travel through cyberspace. Stephen never got back to me. He must be really attached to that *ph*.

To avoid the embarrassment and/or disappointment that may result from prematurely ejaculating our emails, I recommend that **the very last thing we do when writing an email is type in our email recipient's email address.** I am going to write that in bold again: **the very last thing we do when writing an email is type in our email recipient's email address.** This technique alone has been proven to cure 80 percent of all cases of premature email ejaculation.

Before we type in the email recipient's email address, we must make sure everything is perfect. How do we get everything perfect? Well, we have to do something radical, something almost unheard of: we have to PROOFREAD our emails. We must proofread them to make sure they adhere to the email etiquette guideline I am about to tell you all about. If you follow these guidelines, both you and your email recipient are guaranteed to experience a higher level of satisfaction:

The Eight Rules of Email Etiquette

1. Be Smarter Than a Two-Year-Old.

As soon as I graduated from college, off I flitted to Costa Rica for some postcollege self-discovery, thinking I was pretty exceptional for being so free-spirited. It turned out I was more the rule than the exception: the country was full of young women from all over the world in their early twenties with a similar agenda. And, it turned out I wasn't even close to being the most free-spirited. I recall a lovely Norwegian girl who was so free-spirited she bore a beautiful Costa Rican/Norwegian baby girl.

I realized, however, that there was definitely one benefit of raising a child there: the baby ended up speaking Norwegian, Spanish, *and* English. And the most amazing part of it was that she spoke Spanish to her father, Norwegian to her mother, and English to me. I was a little offended; by that time, I had quite a tan—I thought I might be able to pass as a local.

But once I got over my disappointment, I realized how incredible it was that a two-year-old knew to whom to speak which language, considering most of us adults are also trilingual but still can't get that part right.

Yes, most of us are trilingual. We speak English, Slang, and Cyber.

For example, in English we would write

Dear Staff,

I would like to recognize Sarah's outstanding performance.

In Slang we would write

Hey Homies,
Shout out to Sarah for doin' her thing.

In Cyber we would write

dear staff
i wld like 2 ACK sarah 4 her per4manz

These languages, however, are not interchangeable. Feel free to write in Cyber and Slang to friends and family. (Although, Grandma may have no idea what the hell you are talking about.) (Then again, does Grandma even use email?) The point is—in all professional and academic emails, definitely use English.

For example, if you are writing an email to your boss to complain about your nosy cubicle neighbor who always eavesdrops on your conversations, do not tell your boss "Nelly is all up in my Kool-aid." Your boss may reprimand Nelly for stealing your beverage from the staff lounge.

Other helpful hints:

- When asking for a raise, refrain from asking for *more cheddar*. Instead of a larger paycheck, you may receive a Hickory Farms basket.
- When asking whether or not your colleague understands you, refrain from asking "Do ya feel me?" We don't want you brought up on sexual harassment charges.

I would also be careful when using acronyms, **unless you are absolutely positive that your email recipient knows what the letters stand for.** For example, as far as I am concerned **TIA** is the Spanish word for aunt and **IMHO** means that the writer has sex for money.

2. Don't Use Your Porn Name

Do you know how to find your porn name? You combine the name of your first pet and the name of your first street. My porn name is actually perfect for an English major; it's Max Beth. Apparently, in the porn world I've got a kinky Shakespearean thing going on.

Finding your email address name, however, is not quite as straightforward. There's no set formula. Many of us choose to use our first and last names (janesmith@server.com) or our first initial and last name (jsmith@server.com), but there are those of us who want to be a bit more creative. We want our email address to say something about who we are.

This is where it becomes tricky—especially if, like me, you are constantly asking yourself, "Who am I?" Am I the sexy, femme fatale Angelina Jolie type, am I going for the Jennifer Aniston all-American girl thing, or am I into the whole quirky Drew Barrymore image?

During my years of teaching, I have discovered that many of us are definitely opting for the Jenna Jameson. I have received emails from the likes of

cowboywoody69@server.com

cuteasssurferchick@server.com

Latvianhottie@server.com

hotpantz@server.com

I have also discovered that it's difficult to focus on the content of the email from someone with such a sexy name; I find myself a little distracted. (Is it getting hot in here?) Plus, it's difficult to take someone who designates himself Cowboywoody seriously.

Save your sexy email addresses for friends and family. (Although, again, think about poor Grandma.) I highly recommend using some version of the name on your birth certificate as your email address in academic and professional emails.

However, ***do*** continue to use such names as hotpantz and cowboywoody69 if you are applying for a job at Hustler or Chippendales.

Oh, one more thing:

If you have to add a number to your name in your email address (e.g., janesmith456@server.com), I recommend trying **not** to include a zero in the number. It's hard to differentiate the number 0 from the letter O, especially when you jot it down by hand.

3. Say My Name

I didn't realize how attached I was to my name until I started receiving emails from students who did not address me. I mean, if you are going to ask me for an extension on an essay or ask me to reconsider a grade, I'd appreciate a Dear Ms. Baranick, a Dear Professor, or even a Hi Jenny.

We have to remember that an email, unlike instant messaging or texting, is essentially a letter, so in academic or professional communication, we must include a greeting. Here's how to do it:

- **Start out formal**

You know how on a first date women dress up and shave their legs (even above the knee), and then after a couple months, drop the charade: legs return to prickly and the cute dresses become comfy sweats.

Well, email relationships are similar. When I email someone for the first time, I start out formal. For example, if I email a man, I use *Dear Mr. Last Name*:

Dear Mr. Jones: We use a colon when the salutation is formal.

Then, I leave the ball in his court. If he emails me back and addresses me as *Ms. Baranick,* then I continue with the formality, but if he sends back a *Hello Jenny*, then I happily drop the charade and for his next email he gets a

Hello Bob, We use a comma when the salutation is informal.

Note: I wrote "Hello," not "Hey" or "Hi."

Women are more complicated creatures. Unlike men who are always addressed as *Mr.* whether they are married, single, divorced, five years old, or ninety-five, women's marital status dictates whether they are addressed as *Miss, Mrs.,* or *Ms.* So if we are sending an email to a woman we haven't met, we may not know if she's married or not. Even if she is married, are we even sure she took her husband's last name? Or maybe she was once married, but she's not anymore. Or maybe she's married, but she despises her husband and doesn't want to be reminded that she has vowed to live with him 'til death parts them.

To avoid having to hire a private investigator before sending a quick email, it's become common to simply use the title *Ms.* Using *Ms.* demonstrates the respect of using a title without the risk of bringing up any personal issues. For example:

Dear Ms. Anderson:

Even more complicated than how to address women in emails is how to address someone whose name does not indicate one's gender. In addition to the good old gender neutral names, such as Pat and Terry, thanks to celebrities, there is a new generation of offspring with crazy names such as Blue Angel, Audio Science, and Moxie (No, I did not make those up). So what do we do if our boss asks us to shoot an email to Destry Spielberg but leaves to play golf before we can inquire whether Destry is Steven Spielberg's son or daughter? Well, in this case, instead of using a Mr. or Ms., just write out the full name:

Dear Destry Spielberg:

You can also write

Dear Sir or Madam:

But, for some reason, doesn't "Sir or Madam" just seem to rub in the fact that their name is crazy?

4. Show a Little Skin

I receive emails from people trying to sell me Viagra every day; it's as though they think I am married to Hugh Hefner. I donated to Greenpeace once, and now they email me so often I wonder where they find the time to save the whales. Every day, I am emailed credit card offers, offers of friendship from people, and offers of sharing in the fortune of a Nigerian prince. Because of this daily influx of email, it's so important that my students and colleagues give their email a good title in the subject header—to differentiate it from all the crap.

However, when my students do include a title in the subject header of their emails, often they simply write their names. This is not ideal because I have approximately one hundred students per quarter, and I may not recognize their name and confuse it with spam.

For me, the perfect email title is like the perfect first date outfit. It reveals just enough without giving too much away. The perfect email subject title states the main purpose of the email in a few words.

For example, let's say that one of my students has a question about the English Composition homework; then a perfect email title would be:

English Composition Homework

If you are emailing an employer about a job, simply include the job title:

Personal Assistant Position

If you are emailing your boss because you will be missing an important meeting because you have scored some tickets to *Dancing with the Stars*, your email title should be:

Family Emergency

5. But, I Was Just Kidding . . .

We sarcastic folk are often sorely misunderstood. Sometimes we are just trying to be funny, but it gets misconstrued as serious, and we look like big jerks. At least in face-to-face conversation, it's easier to grasp the tone of a conversation; in writing we don't have the other person's tone of voice or facial expressions to use as clues. Consequently, some serious misunderstandings can occur.

We have to take extra precautions in our emails to make sure that nothing can be misinterpreted, and unfortunately that may mean refraining from blessing the email recipient with our wonderful Chandler Bing-like wit.

However, it's not only sarcasm that gets lost in translation in our writing; sometimes we are being serious but the other person interprets it as sarcasm. For example, perhaps we write:

Congratulations on the promotion. I'm sure you'll do great.

This may be misconstrued as:

Congratulations on the promotion (eye roll). I'm sure you'll do great (snicker).

So, although I am old school and don't necessarily love the idea of using LOL (laugh out loud) or happy faces J in emails, I *guess* they're helpful if you want to make sure that your reader knows that your email is lighthearted. It's up to you if you want to use the same symbols as your kindergarten teacher. J

6. Too Much Information

I was flipping through *US Weekly* the other day on my lunch break. My first stop: an article about a celebrity and her new baby. "I love everything she does," the proud mother said of her newborn, "If she does a poop and I have to change the diaper, I love that moment." Wow. Thanks. Couldn't we have just left it at "I love everything she does?" I don't think I'll be finishing this sandwich.

Or how about this marital advice from another celebrity: "When you're in bed and you're married to someone, don't fart under the covers and trap her under the covers, because she gets pissed." I mean, I get it: I find every detail about my life fascinating as well, but not only is that kind of gross, you have to understand that when we pick up a tabloid, that's not the kind of information we're interested in. We only want to know:

- If you are cheating on your wife
- If your wife is cheating on you
- How much plastic surgery you and your wife have had

Similarly, we only want to include relevant information in our emails. Keep them short and to the point. For example, if you are emailing because you can't make it to a meeting on Monday at 2:30, there's no need to explain that you can't make it because your husband *usually* picks up the kids from school on Mondays, but he happens to be getting a vasectomy on this coming Monday. Just express your apologies for being unable to attend due to family matters, and perhaps suggest another meeting time.

7. Parting Is Such Sweet Sorrow

For me, the hardest part of an email is the sign off. I always want to use *Thank you*, but it's not always appropriate. I don't want to *thank* my cable company for overcharging me. So when I can't use *Thank you*, I just choose one of the sign offs from the list below:

Sincerely,

Regards,

Best,

Best Regards,

Warm Regards,

In the case of the cable bill, I would probably choose *Sincerely*, but that's only because I heard that *F#$% off* is not professional.

8. Whip 'em Out

There's nothing better than shopping while a little tipsy. Our inhibitions are lowered, and we find ourselves purchasing that bright pink and yellow scarf that we admired on Kate Moss in *Vogue* but thought to ourselves that we could never pull off. The only problem is when we get home and sober up, the lovely scarf never actually makes it out of the closet onto our bodies. We see it in there staring at us, but we look at it in shame and revert back to our neutral color-wearing selves.

None of us really want to be that person. We'd like to be more adventurous. So, let's get in the habit of actually showing off our shiny, new acquisitions while in a sober state. For example, you've all just accumulated a whole bunch of new accessories. You've got your commas, semicolons, apostrophes, and colons. You've learned the dos and don'ts of capitalization, numbers, and spelling. Strut these lessons all over the email page. You've got it, baby, so flaunt it!

Reality Email

If, like me, you watch reality TV because seeing what train wrecks the contestants are makes you feel better about yourself, then these *Reality Emails* should really boost your confidence. You are about to encounter some real emails from students to their English teacher (me), the teacher who really, really cares about punctuation and grammar. Students sending emails like this to an English teacher seems about as appropriate as auditioning for American Idol while suffering from laryngitis.

But, it's not just the terrible grammar and punctuation that qualifies these emails as train wrecks. Check 'em out:

Contestant #1:

Hi Ms. Baranick! This is T—— from your english composition class. I want to do the extra credit that you mentioned to the class last monday. So if i could receive the topic for the timed write essay that would be great! Thanks! With Lots of Love, T—— G——

Yes, he should have capitalized *English Composition* and *Monday* and *I*. And, yes, he uses too many exclamation points. But, what makes this

Reality Email worthy is the sign-off. It's sweet and, let's face it, who can blame him, but I don't recall that *with lots of love* was included in the list of appropriate ways to sign off from a professional email.

Contestant #2:

> **Omg i love you so much jenny, sorry 4 not replying asap but thank you alot im going to get you a gift now**

Again, no matter how strongly you feel it, don't express your love to your teachers (nor to your clients nor to your colleagues). Plus, I don't believe that he really loves me. If he *really* loved me, there wouldn't be a dozen grammatical errors, he wouldn't have used instant messaging acronyms, he definitely wouldn't have used 4 in place of *for*, and I never did get that gift.

Contestant #3:

> **thank U!**

Really? That's it? You didn't have the energy to capitalize the T or write out the word "you." It's the least you could do after what I did for you. (Although I don't know what that is since you obviously didn't have time to mention it. But, whatever it was, I'm sure it was worth a complete three letter word.)

And, now America, it's time to vote for the winner of American Reality Email:

For Contestant #1, call 1-800-wholelottaluv
For Contestant #2, call 1-800-where'smygift
For Contestant #3, call 1-800-lazythanks

Exercise 15: Train Wrecks

Directions: These are real emails from my students. Only the names have been changed to protect their identity. Identify all of their email etiquette errors in the spaces provided.

Subject Header: Stacy Lawson
<racystacy@aol.com>

Jenny,
I havent gotten the homework due tomorrow and I asked Ashley and she said that she didnt have the questions, or couldnt get them to me when I need them. If you could help me out that would be great.
Thank you
Stacy Lawson

Slang/Cyberspeak

Porn Name

Greeting/Sign-off

Subject Header

Content

Grammar

____

____

Subject Header: Regarding My Failure
<jlambert@server.com>

i am very displeased with failing your class. An I don't agree with your assumption of failure. I would like to review this over in person with you and the director beacuse i don't feel i should have to repeat the course. Thank you and I look forward to speaking to you.

Slang/Cyberspeak

____

____

Porn Name

____

____

Greeting/Sign-off

____

____

Subjcct Header

____

____

Content

____

____

Grammar

____

____

16

Looks Matter: Formatting Academic Papers, Letters, and Résumés

We go around saying things like "you shouldn't judge a book by its cover" and "true beauty is on the inside," but let's cut the crap, shall we? There's a billion-dollar industry that thrives because the hint of a wrinkle is so hideous that we inject poison into our bodies. If that doesn't prove that we're superficial, how about the fact that Leonardo diCaprio keeps dating models and not English teachers.

I'll admit it. I'm totally superficial. When I was in high school, I plastered my wall with pictures of Johnny Depp, not Bill Gates. I wear high heels to make my legs appear longer even though I'm sure sneakers are better for my feet. Hell, I even judge my students based on appearance.

Now, I don't judge them based on *their* personal appearance, but I can't help but judge them based on how their essays look.

Put yourself in my shoes (my four-inch stilettos) and imagine receiving an essay that is crinkled and has coffee stains all over it. Instead of having been neatly stapled, the upper left-hand corner of the essay has been carelessly folded, and the last two paragraphs are barely legible because the printer started running out of ink. I don't look at the essay and think, "Wow! I love this bohemian approach to writing in which all formalities of appearance have been sacrificed. When this essay inevitably breaks free from the shackles of its loosely folded corner, I can't wait to search all over for the missing page and then try to reconstruct the essay in the correct order because this avant-garde student forewent the banal tradition of including page numbers." This essay could have been written by the next Hemingway, but my heart has already hardened against the student who showed respect neither to me nor to the assignment.

Résumés

R-E-S-P-E-C-T. Find out what it means to me. Actually, I'm not really the one you should be worried about. You see, I am a mere teacher. Sure, I am in control of your grade, but that's not where the real power lies. The real power lies in the hands of those who control your money-making potential, and I am afraid there are quite a few people who don't realize how important it is that the written material that can affect their careers (i.e., job applications, résumés, cover letters, and proposals) looks good.

Based on résumé looks alone, which one would you hire?

Edward Cullens

Forks, WA 98331

Cell: 976-SUCK

Email: sparklevamp@vmail.com

QUALIFICATIONS:

- Don't sleep
- Piano virtuoso
- Completed medical school twice
- Sparkle in the sunlight
- Immortal
- Did I mention that I sparkle

EXPERIENCE:

2009 ***Breaking Dawn*** ***Forks, WA*** ***Vampire***

- Fathered and delivered a half -human baby
- *Finally turned Bella into a vampire.*
- *Sparkled*

2008 Eclipse Forks, WA

Vampire

- Proved teamwork skills by working with werewolves.
- Defeated more vampires.
- Sparkled

2007 New moon Italy Vampire

- Sacrificed happiness to save Bella
- Sparkled
- Moped

2005 Twilight Forks, WA Vampire

- ***Saved Bella by stopping a car with bare hands***
- ***Fell in love with Bella***
- ***Studied biology***
- ***Saved Bella from turning into a vampire***
- ***Sparkled***

Jacob Black

Forks, WA 98331

Cell: 976-WOLF

Email: were@wolfmail.com

QUALIFICATIONS:

- Boast incredible abs
- Can shape shift into a werewolf
- Can repair automobiles
- Have high body temperature
- Experience delayed aging

EXPERIENCE:

2009 ***Breaking Dawn Forks, WA***

- *Werewolf*
- Helped deliver Bella and Edward's child
- Imprinted Bella and Edward's child
- Displayed glorious abs

2008 ***Eclipse Forks, WA***

- *Werewolf*
- Kissed Bella against her will
- Kissed a willing Bella
- Displayed glorious abs

2007 ***New Moon Forks, WA***

- *Werewolf*
- Hunted vampires
- Fell in love with Bella
- Saved Bella from drowning
- Displayed glorious abs

2005 Twilight Forks, WA

- *Werewolf*
- Tried to warn Bella about Edward
- Wore a terrible wig
- Displayed glorious abs

In addition to urging you to be obsessed with looks, I am also going to suggest that you conform. I know. I know. Robert Frost took the road less traveled by and it made all the difference. Pink Floyd warns against becoming just another brick in the wall. Paris Hilton said, "Life is too short to blend in." However, when writing essays, résumés, proposals, and the like, I urge you to make sure your document conforms to the prescribed format.

Papers and Essays

Let's talk about academic essays for a moment. Depending on the discipline you're studying, you will most likely be required to write your essay according to a particular format. The most popular formats are MLA, APA, and Chicago Style. Since I teach English, my students are required to use MLA format. This is what it looks like:

> Isabella Swan
> Professor Baranick
> English Composition
> 5 February 2012
>
> Vampires vs. Werewolves
>
> There are many difficult choices we have to make in our lifetimes. We have to decide between Coke and Pepsi and Britney and Christina. But the biggest decision I've ever had to make was between a vampire and a werewolf. At first, it didn't seem like a tough decision; I was vampire all the way. But

No, it's not sexy. The font, font-size, and spacing are uniform. The header provides basic information. If it were clothes, it would be khaki pants. But the header provides all the information I need, the double-spacing and margins leave me room to write comments, the font is legible, and it looks so nice and neat. (Let me just change that grade from a B to a B+.)

If I didn't require my essays to conform to a format, I guarantee you that this is what I'd receive:

Bella

Virgo

"Vampires vs. Werewolves"

There are many difficult choices we have to make in our lifetimes. We have to decide between Coke and Pepsi and Britney and Christina. But the biggest decision I've ever had to make was between a vampire and a werewolf. At first, it didn't seem like a tough decision; I was vampire all the way. But

I promise that making sure word documents conform to a prescribed format does not stifle creativity. The content can still be wonderfully creative. In fact, this nice, boring format enables the content to be the focus, not the crazy font or the spacing. And my favorite part is that it shows me that the student took the time to make their essay conform to the format I requested. Yes, that's right; I am an egotistical, tyrannical control-freak.

But, I am not the only one. Other egotistical, tyrannical control-freaks include your prospective employers, your bosses, and your potential investors, so when constructing your résumés and business proposals, make sure that they're nice and neat. Check out one of the various websites or guidebooks regarding proper formatting. Make sure all your bullet points line up perfectly. Make sure your font size is consistent. Make sure your spacing is uniform. Don't bold and italicize randomly.

And then once you work your way up to CEO or own your own company, you can impose your own tyrannical requirements on others.

Cover Letters

Unlike the paragraph formatting guidelines for a paper or essay, the paragraphs in a letter should be single spaced and should not be indented. Instead, skip a line space between paragraphs.

EXERCISE 16: HELP WANTED

Directions: Below are the requirements for how to format a cover letter. After reviewing the requirements, identify the formatting errors in Count Dracula's cover letter.

Requirements:

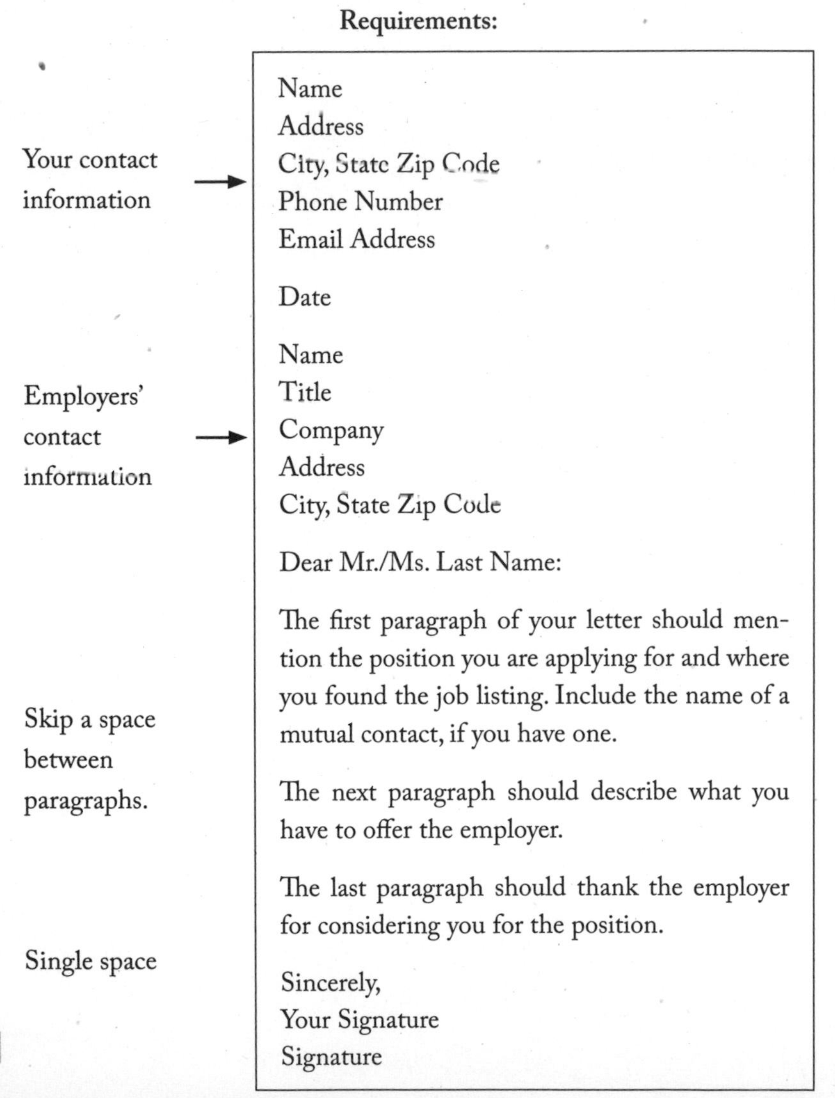

Stephenie Meyer
C/O Little, Brown and Company
237 Park Avenue
New York, NY 1001

Count Dracula
Bran Castle
Str. Traian Mosoiu 24
Bran, Transylvania 401167

Dear Countess Meyer,

I am applying for a role in your next Vampire novel. I know you are not writing another vampire novel at the moment, but you should because you made millions with your first series. I would be the perfect candidate for a new vampire series because it's been over 100 years since Bram Stoker wrote that book about me, and people are sick of sparkle boy—they're ready for some new vampire blood.

I have superhuman strength. I can shapeshift into a bat and a wolf. Did you hear that Cullen? A bat AND a wolf! I can read minds and control the weather.
Thank you for considering me for this delicious position. I look forward to hearing from you. (I hear your blood type is ABO—my favrorite.)

Bloodiest regards,

Count Dracula

17

Textual Healing: Proofreading

It happens even to the best of relationships. After a while, you find yourself in a rut. It's not that you don't care anymore, but after doing things the same way for so long, you don't even remember how to approach your partner in a different way. And be honest: you probably have become a little lazy and don't put in the effort you used to. You probably don't spend as much time as you should focusing on the little things that nurture a relationship and help it blossom.

I know that when that happens in my relationships, I like to invite another person into the mix. This can really add some fresh perspective and excitement to the current relationship. This person won't only provide inspiration but also insight into the strengths and weaknesses of your techniques. That's why when my relationship between me and my writing gets a bit stagnant I always have someone else proofread my work.

You see, when we proofread our own writing, it's difficult to catch the errors. We know what we are trying to say, so we overlook the typos and believe the content flows beautifully and makes perfect sense. Therefore, a great way to catch our errors and ensure that we are communicating our message clearly to our reader is to have someone else proofread it for us.

Threesomes are tricky, though. It's important to invite someone in who you trust with you and your writing. It's also a waste of time to invite someone in who isn't as good if not better than you when it comes to the written word. Also, a third party may not be available right when we need him or her. In reality, sometimes it's just going to be you and your writing. If that happens to be the case, don't worry. Here are some tips about how to enhance your text life:

Don't make it a quickie

Quickies have their charm; however, most of the time, what one partner considers a "quickie," the other partner considers the most unsatisfying two minutes of her life. Now, I'm not saying we have to wine and dine our writing, but when we proofread, a quick glance is pointless.

Honor your refractory period

A refractory period is defined as the amount of time it takes for an excitable membrane to be ready for a second stimulus once it returns to its resting state following excitation. Let's be frank: there are few things more exciting to our membranes than writing. Writing stimulates our brains to penetrate language, conjugate verbs, and insert punctuation. Therefore, it's a good idea to take a nice long rest in between writing and proofreading. If we try to proofread immediately after we complete our writing, our proofreading will most likely be a bit flaccid.

Make sure it's hard

Although it requires wasting wood, I have found that I discover more errors if I proofread a hard copy of my work rather than an electronic copy.

Make stimulating conversation—out loud

"You're a naughty little sentence! I am going to punctuate you all night long!"

That's not exactly what I had in mind when I said stimulating conversation, but if you're into that kind of thing, go for it.

I've realized that people find themselves quite stimulating, so it can really enhance your relationship if you take the time to listen to your partner. However, since your written document can't actually talk to you, why don't you read it out loud? By hearing the words out loud, you might discover important qualities about your writing that you never noticed before—like the fact that it contains some run-on sentences.

Try a different position

I realize that I don't know you, but I bet you always do it the same way: I bet you always proofread starting with the first sentence and ending with the last. Why not add a little bit of spice to your proofreading and do it doggy style? Start with the last sentence and end with the first. This will allow you to experience your writing from a different perspective so you won't just go into autopilot as you proofread. You will probably realize that your writing is even naughtier than you thought. And when I say naughty, I mean not as grammatically chaste.

Get hard core

If you thought proofreading your writing doggy style was hard core, then the next two techniques I am about to introduce might be too much for you. These techniques are only for those who really want to make writing errors their bitch. These techniques involve some dark psychological tricks. If that sounds like something you're into, get your whip and follow me.

The first technique is to break down your writing only to build it back up again. Click return after every sentence until your entire document is broken down into lines of stand-alone sentences; then proofread each sentence individually. Seeing each sentence suspended there, vulnerable to our scrutiny without all those other sentences around them to mask their errors, we might just find that our sentences were not as strong as we thought. Only after we whip each sentence into shape can we reassemble them into the integrated document they once were.

The next hard-core technique is something I picked up in college. A friend of mine was in a sorority, and as part of the hazing ritual, the existing sorority members made the new members strip down, and they circled all of their bodily "imperfections." Brutal, huh? Well, I am suggesting an even more psychologically brutal attack on our writing. Instead of just circling the errors, go through the document and circle every single punctuation mark. Then evaluate each mark one by one to decide if they really belong.

Exercise 17: Heal That Text

Directions: The following passage has that feeling. It needs textual healing. It's time to put those proofreading techniques to work.

We're all busy most of us are probably balancing a job and a family, a job and school, or two mistresses and a wife. i know its hard. But it's important that we find some time to nurture our relationship with our-writing. Studies show that even many highly educated, college-graduated professionals don't possess basik writing skills that businesses want. Therefore, in order to make sure were a strong candidate for our dream job we should take steps to strengthen our writing relationship. When Im looking for relationship-strengthening tips, i always turn to *cosmopolitan* magazine. Here's how *Cosmopolitan* suggests we strengthen relationships watch porn together, nibble earlobes, and wear thigh-highs. So there you go! If we don't spend this quality time with our writing, well very likely end up spelling words incorrectly, capitalizing the wrong words, misusing our colons and apostrophes, and, worst of all, missing our periods

Answer Key

EXERCISE 1: GOOGLE ME THIS

Y	O	U	R		T	H	E	R	E		T	H	A	N	
O											H		F		
U	S	E	D			L		L	O	S	E		F		
'				T	O	O					I		E		
R			W			O					R		C		
E	F	F	E	C	T	S						I	T	'	S
			A			E						T			U
			T									S			P
			H												P
			E												O
			R												S
													L	I	E
															D

Exercise 2: How to Choose the Right Relationship

1. If polygamy is, in fact, becoming more acceptable (nowadays/now a days), would you grab some more spouses?
2. I might get seven spouses so I can have a new one for (everyday/every day) of the week.
3. I wonder if my spouses would get jealous of (eachother/each other).
4. One relationship is (alot/a lot) of work; imagine dealing with seven.
5. At least I would finally be (apart/a part) of a big family.

Exercise 3: Catch Them If You Can

Once upon a time, a beautiful woman, who claimed to be a princess, sought shelter in a prince's castle on a rainy night. The prince thought she was so hot he would of married her irregardless of whether or not she descended from royalty. The prince's mother, on the other hand, wanted to keep the bloodline pure so her descendants could forever distinguish themselves from mere commoners. So to test the "princess," the queen placed a pea under the twenty mattresses that made up the bed on which the "princess" would sleep. Apparently, real princesses have the sensitivity to feel the pea. In the morning, when asked about her night's sleep, the "princess" said that she would of slept better if it weren't for something hard in the bed. Everyone at the table had to stop theirselves from laughing because she said "something hard in the bed," and they all had dirty minds. Anyways, she went on to show them a pea-size welt on her back, and the prince rejoiced because from now on he was going to be that "something hard in the bed."

EXERCISE 4: OH, HOW YOU DO RUN-ON!

I had the strangest dream last night. I was in my house but it wasn't really *my* house; it was a mansion filled with balloons. On the couch was this guy wearing a pirate shirt sitting whispering sweet nothings in my ear. I looked up to see it was Johnny Depp. He told me he wanted me to star in the next *Pirates of the Caribbean* with him. He promised that after we finished shooting the movie we would sail away and live happily ever after. I was so excited that I would finally have the opportunity to wear my eye patch. I packed my suitcase and was about to join Johnny; then I heard my mom's voice telling me that I couldn't go anywhere until I did the dishes.

*Answers may vary, but I thought only two semicolons were appropriate.

EXERCISE 5A: BREAKING UP IS HARD TO DO

1. Lloyd Dobler was desperate to win back Diane Court and blasted a Peter Gabriel love song outside her bedroom window. No comma
2. Alexandra did not cope well with being jilted by Dan, and she boiled his daughter's bunny.
3. Rhett told Scarlett that he didn't give a damn and walked out the door. No comma
4. Joel couldn't cope with his breakup and had every memory from the relationship erased from his mind. No comma
5. Jack Berger didn't want to date Carrie Bradshaw anymore, and he communicated this to her on a Post-it note.

Exercise 5b: The Other Kind of FANBOYS

1. I felt like I would never be good enough for him, for it's impossible to compete with Princess Leia in the golden bikini.
2. We would have gone to the prom, but the big comic book convention was on the same weekend.
3. He kept all of his Star Wars action figures in their original packaging so he could sell them for millions of dollars one day. No comma
4. He tried to learn to speak Vulcan but never quite mastered it. No comma
5. He wanted his ears to look like Spock's, so he slept with clothespins on the tips of his ears for a year.

Exercise 5c: Make a Good Impression

Answers will vary.

Exercise 5d: Did You Really Need to Tell Me That?

1. Richard, who has three nipples, just got hired at my work.
2. The dress I let you borrow to wear on your date, the one I wore when I made out with Steve in the back of the car, needs to be dry-cleaned.
3. I'd like to introduce you to the nice girl who held my hair for me when I vomited at the club the other night. No commas
4. I have a thing for men who have outie belly buttons. No commas
5. Eddie's stand-up comedy routine last night, which made me laugh so hard I peed a little bit in my pants, was his best one yet.

Exercise 6: Have Some Self-Respect

1. Jane went on a blind date with her coworker's brother Sam, who took her to meet his parents on their first date.
2. During Kevin's first date with Alicia, she talked about her last three ex-boyfriends' penis size.
3. Lola seemed great, but Kevin got suspicious when he saw her walk into the men's bathroom.
4. _______________ dating experiences were equally disastrous.

B. Kevin's and Jane's

5. They both decided to revise their _______________ on eHarmony.

A. profiles

Exercise 7: Renaissance Men

1. Einstein did more than discover the theory of relativity. Even though he was married to Elsa, he also did Estella, Ethel, Toni, and his "Russian spy lover," Margarita. No colon
2. Daniel Radcliffe will probably always be known as the guy who played Harry Potter, but I will remember him for a different role: the one in the play *Equus* in which he played a naked stable boy who had an obsession with horses.
3. Bill Clinton will go down in history for not having sexual relations with Monica Lewinsky, but he also accomplished other important feats: he was the governor of Arkansas and the 42nd president of the United States.
4. To me, Ozzy Osbourne will always be the guy who bit the head off a bat, but he seems to have a softer side since his favorite TV shows as a child were reportedly *I Love Lucy*, *Lassie,* and *Roy Rogers*. No colon
5. And here's one final Richard Gere fact: he was also a phenomenal gymnast.

Exercise 8: Somebody's Been . . .

1. Somebody's been drinking—and I mean really drinking—my vodka.
2. Somebody's been watching my dirty movie collection.
   You didn't put a hyphen between dirty and movie, did you? That would mean I collect pornography. My movie collection has just been collecting a bit of dust. Sheesh!
3. Somebody's been sleeping in my water bed.
   No hyphen

4. Somebody's been eating my Ben and Jerry's ice cream—all three tubs.
5. Somebody's been reading my self-help books.

Exercise 9: Give Her a Rest

My schedule is up in the air at the moment. I am in town for sure until early September, but my grandma's 80th is in early October so I will probably be back in New York for that week. Then after that I am not sure; I'm trying to figure that out. My lease will be up so I'm trying to figure out where to live, but I would love to see you if our schedules permit.

Exercise 10: Trouble in Paradise

1. Gilligan may be your "little buddy," but I just heard him call you a "big jerk."
2. Can you believe that Mary Ann said in front of everyone, "Ginger's coconuts are fake"?
3. Gilligan sure had nerve when he told Mary Ann, "The Professor learned all his tricks from me"!
4. I just heard Ginger ask Mrs. Howell, "Don't you think wearing such tight shorts in such a hot climate would result in Mary Ann getting some kind of, you know, infection?"
5. The Skipper just hollered to the Professor, "Wait for me, little buddy!"

Exercise 11: If I Were a Rich Girl . . .

1. I would go to the Westin Hotel in New York City and order their $1000 bagel. It is topped with white truffle cream cheese and infused with goji berries and golden leaves.

2. I would find the person who bought the pair of Stuart Weitzman shoes from Harrods in London for $1.5 million and offer them $2 million. How could I not? The shoes are woven from platinum and set with 626 rubies. Plus, they were inspired by my favorite movie, *The Wizard of Oz*.
3. To go with my new sparkly shoes, I would blow $5 million on the new bra from Victoria's Secret called The Black Diamond Fantasy Miracle Bra.
4. To deal with the harsh autumn and winter months we experience in Southern California, I would buy a $50,000 crocodile skin umbrella.
5. Since I love vacationing in the Bahamas, Hawaii, and Jamaica, I would buy my own island. And I'm in luck. The island Vatu Varu, located in Fiji, is on sale for the reasonable price of $40 million.

Exercise 12: Stop Projecting

1. When they first meet me, the first thing they notice is [answers will vary].

The answer must be *they* because *meet* and *notice* are plural verbs and will only agree with a plural pronoun.

2. [could be either He, She, or They] would be surprised by my ability to [answers will vary].
3. If someone had met me five years ago, he or she would have noticed my [answers will vary].

The answer must be the singular pronoun because *someone* is singular and is gender neutral.

4. When people first learn that I'm [answers will vary], they tend to react by [answers will vary].

The answer must be *they* because *people* is plural and requires a plural pronoun.

5. It's better if they don't interrupt me when I'm [answers will vary]; if they do, I might [answers will vary].

The answer must be *they* because *don't* is a plural verb and requires a plural pronoun.

Exercise 13: Lie to Me

1. I have ____________________ Facebook friends.

Answers will vary.

2. ____________________ people asked me for my autograph on the way here.

Answers will vary, but the number must be written out.

3. I can bench press ____________________ pounds.

Answers will vary, but the number must be expressed as a numeral.

4. My favorite decade is the ____________________.

Answers will vary, but make sure the answer is apostrophe free.

5. I kissed ____________________ people this year compared with ____________________ people last year.

Answers will vary, but both numbers either have to be written out or both numbers have to be expressed as numerals.

Exercise 14: Bust It Up

1. Answers will vary.
2. *Well* (unless you're ballsy)
3. A
4. A
5. A. Any of the following are correct: *and, furthermore, moreover*
   B. Any of the following are correct: *but, however, nonetheless*

Exercise 15: Train Wrecks

Subject Header: Stacy Lawson
<racystacy@aol.com>

Jenny,

I havent gotten the homework due tomorrow cuz I asked Amy and she said that she didnt have the questions, or couldnt get them to me when I need them. If you could help me out that would be great.

Thank you
Stacy Lawson

Slang/Cyberspeak

I'm not her *cuz*.

Porn name

By *racy*, I'm assuming she meant that she raced through this email *cuz* she forgot a couple of apostrophes and commas.

Greeting/Sign-off

I let my students use my first name, but it would have been nice if she said *hello*.

Subject Header

You guys wouldn't know this, but I have Stacy in two of my classes. Thus, it would have been better if she included the course name in the Subject Header because I have no idea what homework she's talking about.

Content

Which one is it? Did Amy not have the questions or could Amy not get them to you? Stacy's inconsistency leads me to believe that either she didn't really ask Amy or she procrastinated and asked too late.

Grammar

Are apostrophes too much to ask?

Subject Header: Regarding My Failure
<jlambert@server.com>

i am very displeased with failing your class. An I don't agree with your assumption of failure. I would like to review this over in person with you and the director beacuse i don't feel i should have to repeat the course. Thank you and I look forward to speaking to you.

Slang/Cyberspeak

All clear

Porn name

Porn free

Greeting/Parting

You'd think he'd want to butter me up a little bit with a *Dear Highly Esteemed Professor*.

Also, by failing to sign off, it's like he stormed away in anger and slammed the door in my face.

Subject Header

Regarding your failure in what? Life? Past relationships? Choosing the winning lottery numbers?

Content

My ASSUMPTION of your failure! Sweetheart, grades aren't based on assumptions, nor are they based on your feelings. Because you insulted my judgment, I assume you won't be taking MY class next quarter when you have to repeat this course.

Grammar

Refuting a failing grade in English with this grammar is as effective as refuting a drunk driving ticket while swigging from a bottle of Jack Daniels.

Exercise 16: Help Wanted

This should be Dracula's contact information. →

The date is missing. →

This should be the prospective employers' contact information. →

Too much space. →

The comma following her name should be a colon. →

The font is crazy. →

Need a space between these two paragraphs. →

Too much space between last paragraph and sign-off. →

Stephenie Meyer
C/O Little, Brown and Company
237 Park Avenue
New York, NY 1001

Count Dracula
Bran Castle
Str. Traian Mosoiu 24
Bran, Transylvania 401167

Dear Ms. Meyer,

I am applying for a role in your next Vampire novel. I know you are not writing another vampire novel at the moment, but you should because you made millions with your first series. I would be the perfect candidate for a new vampire series because it's been over 100 years since Bram Stoker wrote that book about me, and people are sick of sparkle boy—they're ready for some new vampire blood.

I have superhuman strength. I can shapeshift into a bat and a wolf. Did you hear that Cullen? A bat AND a wolf! I can read minds and control the weather.
Thank you for considering me for this delicious position. I look forward to hearing from you. (I hear your blood type is ABO—my favrorite.)

Bloodiest regards,

Count Dracula

Exercise 17: Heal That Text

We're all busy. Most of us are probably balancing a job and a family, a job and school, or two mistresses and a wife. I know it's hard. But it's important that we find some time to nurture our relationship with our writing. Studies show that even many highly educated, college-graduated professionals don't possess basic writing skills that businesses want. Therefore, in order to make sure we're a strong candidate for our dream job, we should take steps to strengthen our writing relationship. When I'm looking for relationship-strengthening tips, I always turn to *Cosmopolitan* magazine. Here's how *Cosmopolitan* suggests we strengthen relationships: watch porn together, nibble earlobes, and wear thigh-highs. So there you go! If we don't spend this quality time with our writing, we'll very likely end up spelling words incorrectly, capitalizing the wrong words, misusing our colons and apostrophes, and, worst of all, missing our periods.

References

"Affleck." *Urban Dictionary*. 2012. Web. 17 May 2012.

"Celebrity *Real Names*." Zelo.com. 1996-2012. Web. 17 May 2012.

"Cougar." *Merriam-Webster.com*. Merriam-Webster, 2012. Web. 17 May 2012.

Dictionary.com. 2012. Web. 17 May 2012.

Fogarty, Mignon. "Good Versus Well." *Grammar Girl Quick and Dirty Tips for Better Writing*. 20 April 2007. Web. 17 May 2012.

"Grammar Myths." *Grammarphobia.com*. 2003. Web. 17 May 2012.

Hacker, Diana, and Nancy Sommers. *A Pocket Style Manual*. 6th ed, Boston: Bedford/St. Martins, 2012. Print.

Hilton, Paris. *Confessions of an Heiress: A Tongue-in-Chic Peek Behind the Pose*. New York: Fireside, 2004. Print.

"Longest English Sentence." *Wikipedia: The Free Encyclopedia*. Wikimedia Foundation, Inc. 11 May 2012. Web. 17 May 2012.

"New letters shed light on Einstein's love life." *MSNBC.com*. 2012. Web. 17 May 2012.

"Ozzy Osbourne Bio." *Celebrity Gossip*. 2012. Web. 17 May 2012.

Strumpf, Michael, and Auriel Douglas. *The Grammar Bible: Everything You Always Wanted to Know About Grammar but Didn't Know Whom to Ask*. New York: Owl Book, 2004. Print.

Index